THE
NAVY DIRECTORY
2018

Compiled on the 01 January 2019

D1464516

a Williams Lea company

Published by TSO (The Stationery Office), part of Williams Lea,
and available from:

Online
www.tsoshop.co.uk

Mail, Telephone, Fax & E-mail
TSO
PO Box 29, Norwich, NR3 1GN
Telephone orders/General enquiries: 0333 202 5070
Fax orders: 0333 202 5080
E-mail: customer.services@tso.co.uk
Textphone 0333 202 5077

TSO@Blackwell and other Accredited Agents

First printed edition published 2019
ISBN 9780117731387

Printed in the United Kingdom for The Stationery Office
J003574908   c0.7   07/19

PREFACE

This edition of the Navy Directory has been produced largely from the information held within the Ministry of Defence's "Joint Personnel and Administration" system (JPA) as at 01 January 2019.

Officers who succeed to peerages, baronetcies or courtesy titles should notify their Career Manager.

Serving officers who notice errors relating to their data in the Navy Directory should ensure that the data held within JPA is accurate & up to date. If you are unable to make these corrections within your JPA account, you should seek assistance either from your JPA administrator or Career Manager. All other errors or omissions should be brought to the attention of the Editor of the Navy Directory. Readers who should wish to comment on this edition of the Navy Directory are invited to write to:

> The Editor of the Navy Directory
> Mail Point 2.2
> West Battery
> Whale Island
> PORTSMOUTH
> PO2 8DX

In order to satisfy the United Nations Convention on the Law of the Sea (UNCLOS) the details of those commanding a warship are published on the RN Website. Due to the wide-availability of the Navy Directory on the Defence Intranet and the RN Website, free distribution of the Navy Directory in hard copy format has ceased.

iv

CONTENTS

MEMBERS OF THE ROYAL FAMILY

HIS ROYAL HIGHNESS THE PRINCE PHILIP, DUKE OF EDINBURGH, KG, KT, OM, GCVO, GBE, ONZ, QSO, AK, GCL, CC, CMM

Lord High Admiral of The United Kingdom..10 Jun 11
Admiral of the Fleet ....15 Jan 53
Admiral of the Fleet Royal Australian Navy .... 1 Apr 54
Admiral of the Fleet Royal New Zealand Navy...15 Jan 53
Admiral of the Royal Canadian Sea Cadets...15 Jan 53
Admiral of the Royal Canadian Navy ....Jun 11

HIS ROYAL HIGHNESS THE PRINCE OF WALES, KG, KT, GCB, OM, AK, QSO, PC, ADC

Admiral of the Fleet ....16 Jun 12
Commodore-in-Chief, Her Majesty's Naval Base, Plymouth .... 8 Aug 06
Admiral of the Fleet Royal New Zealand Navy... 3 Aug 15
Commodore-in-Chief Canada Fleet Atlantic .... 3 May 15

HIS ROYAL HIGHNESS THE DUKE OF CAMBRIDGE, KG, KT, ADC

Lieutenant Commander ....1 Jan 16
Commodore-in-Chief Scotland.. Aug 06
Commodore-in-Chief Submarines .... Aug 06

HIS ROYAL HIGHNESS THE DUKE OF SUSSEX, KCVO, ADC

Lieutenant Commander .... 14 May 18
Captain General, Royal Marines .... 19 Dec 17
Commodore-in-Chief Small Ships and Diving .... Aug 06

HIS ROYAL HIGHNESS THE DUKE OF YORK, KG, GCVO, ADC

Vice Admiral .... 19 Feb 15
Admiral of the Sea Cadet Corps.. 11 May 92
Commodore-in-Chief Fleet Air Arm.. Aug 06

HIS ROYAL HIGHNESS THE EARL OF WESSEX KG, GCVO, ADC

Commodore ....1 Jan 11
Commodore-in-Chief Royal Fleet Auxiliary .... Aug 06

HER ROYAL HIGHNESS THE PRINCESS ROYAL, KG, KT, GCVO, QSO

Admiral Chief Commandant for Women in the Royal Navy .... 15 Aug 12
Commodore-in-Chief, Her Majesty's Naval Base Portsmouth .... Aug 06
Commodore-in-Chief (Fleet Pacific) Royal Canadian Navy..3 May 15

HER ROYAL HIGHNESS THE DUCHESS OF CORNWALL, GCVO

Commodore-in-Chief Naval Medical Services .... Aug 06
Commodore-in-Chief Naval Chaplaincy Services.. 2 Oct 08

HIS ROYAL HIGHNESS PRINCE MICHAEL OF KENT, GCVO

Honorary Vice Admiral Royal Naval Reserve .... 9 Mar 15
Commodore-in-Chief Maritime Reserves .... Aug 06

HER ROYAL HIGHNESS PRINCESS ALEXANDRA THE HON. LADY OGILVY, KG, GCVO

Patron, Queen Alexandra's Royal Naval Nursing Service .... 12 Nov 55

VICE ADMIRAL OF THE UNITED KINGDOM

Honorary Vice Admiral Sir Donald Gosling KCVO RNR .... 2 Apr 12

PERSONAL AIDES-DE-CAMP TO THE QUEEN

Admiral His Royal Highness The Prince of Wales, KG, KT, GCB, OM, AK, QSO, PC, ADC
Lieutenant Commander His Royal Highness The Duke of Cambridge KG, KT, ADC
Lieutenant Commander His Royal Highness The Duke of Sussex KCVO, ADC
Vice Admiral His Royal Highness The Duke of York, KG, GCVO, ADC
Commodore His Royal Highness The Earl of Wessex, KG, GCVO, ADC
Vice Admiral Sir Tim Laurence, KCVO, CB, ADC

PRINCIPAL NAVAL AIDE-DE-CAMP TO THE QUEEN

Admiral Sir Philip Jones KCB ADC .... 08 April 16

NAVAL AND MARINE AIDES-DE-CAMP TO THE QUEEN

Commodore P Coulson ADC .... Appointed 25 Jun 18 Seniority 07 Dec 15
Commodore J G Higham OBE ADC .... Appointed 09 Jan 18 Seniority 23 Mar 15
Brigadier H J White ADC .... Appointed 12 Sep 17 Seniority 05 Sep 17
Captain J R A Woodard ADC .... Appointed 01 Aug 17 Seniority 09 Sep 13

EXTRA NAVAL AND MARINE EQUERRIES TO THE QUEEN

Vice Admiral Sir Tom Blackburn KCVO, CB
Vice Admiral Tony Johnstone-Burt CB OBE
Rear Admiral Sir John Garnier KCVO, CBE
Rear Admiral Sir Robert Woodard KCVO
Commodore A J C Morrow CVO

NAVAL AND MARINE RESERVE AIDES-DE-CAMP TO THE QUEEN

Commodore M E Quinn ADC Ret'd .... Appointed 01 Aug 16 Seniority 28 Apr 16
Commodore D G Elford OBE ADC Ret'd .... Appointed 01 Nov 17 Seniority 01 Jul 13
Captain P Waterhouse ADC Ret'd .... Appointed 28 Apr 17 Seniority 03 Sep 13
Colonel G W Fraser MBE ADC Ret'd .... Appointed 01 Aug 17 Seniority 15 Jul 15
Acting Capt Smith Ret'd .... Appointed 07 Jul 2012 Seniority 30 Jun 06

HONORARY APPOINTMENTS

HONORARY CHAPLAINS TO THE QUEEN

The Reverend Monsignor Andrew McFadden QHC PhB STL VG
The Reverend Tim Wilkinson QHC BA
The Reverend Michael Sharkey QHC

HONORARY PHYSICIANS TO THE QUEEN

Surgeon Commodore A.S. Hughes, QHP, MBChB, MRCGP

HONORARY SURGEON TO THE QUEEN

Surgeon Vice Admiral A J Walker, CB, OBE, QHS, FRCS
Surgeon Captain J G Sharpley, QHS, MRCPSYCH, RN
Surgeon Commodore S W S Millar, QHS, MRCGP, RN

HONORARY DENTAL SURGEON TO THE QUEEN

Surgeon Captain (D) D J Hall, QHDS, BDS, MGDSRCS (Ed), FFGDP(UK), RN

HONORARY NURSE TO THE QUEEN

Commodore I.J. Kennedy, CBE, QHNS, QARNNS
Captain A J Hofman QHNS, QARNNS

HONORARY OFFICERS IN HER MAJESTY'S FLEET

ADMIRAL

His Majesty King Carl XVI Gustaf of Sweden, KG ....25 Jun 75
His Majesty Sultan Haji Hussanal Bolkiah Mu'izzaddin Waddaulah Sultan and Yang Di-pertuan of
Brunei Darussalam, GCB, GCMG .... 4 Aug 01

HONORARY OFFICERS IN HER MAJESTY'S ROYAL MARINES

COLONEL

His Majesty King Harald V of Norway, KG, GCVO ....18 Mar 81

DEFENCE COUNCIL 2018

The Rt Hon
Gavin Williamson CBE MP
Secretary of State for Defence

The Rt Hon
Earl Howe MP
Minister of State for Defence, Deputy Leader of the House of Lords

Stephen Lovegrove
Permanent Secretary for the Ministry of Defence

Admiral Sir Philip Jones KCB ADC
First Sea Lord and Chief of Naval Staff

Air Chief Marshal Sir Stephen Hillier KCB CBE DFC ADC MA RAF
Chief of the Air Staff

General Sir Nick Carter KCB CBE DSO ADC Gen
Chief of the Defence Staff

General Sir Gordon Messenger KCB DSO* OBE ADC
Vice Chief of the Defence Staff

General Sir Chris Deverell KCB MBE ADC Gen
Commander of Joint Forces Command

Cat Little
Director General Finance

THE ADMIRALTY BOARD

Chairman

RT HON GAVIN WILLIAMSON CBE MP
(Secretary of State for Defence)
(Chairman of the Defence Council and Chairman of the
Admiralty Board of the Defence Council)

RT HON MARK LANCASTER TD VR MP
(Minister of State for the Armed Forces)

STUART ANDREW MP
(Minister for Defence Procurement)

RT HON TOBIAS ELWOOD TD, MP
(Minister for Defence Personnel and Veterans)

THE RT HON THE EARL HOWE, PC,
(Minister of State for Defence and the Lords Spokesman on Defence)

STEPHEN LOVEGROVE CB
(Permanent Secretary of the Ministry of Defence)

ADMIRAL SIR PHILIP JONES KCB, ADC
(First Sea Lord and Chief of Naval Staff)

VICE ADMIRAL BEN KEY CBE
(Fleet Commander)

VICE ADMIRAL TONY RADAKIN CB
(Second Sea Lord and Deputy Chief of Naval Staff)

REAR ADMIRAL NICK HINE
(Assistant Chief of Naval Staff)

(Finance Director (Navy))

KEY PERSONNEL – NAVY COMMAND HEADQUARTERS

4* NAVY COMMAND

Chief of Naval Staff/First Sea Lord
Admiral Sir Philip Jones KCB ADC

3* NAVY COMMAND

Second Sea Lord & Deputy Chief of Naval Staff
Vice Admiral B J Key CBE

Fleet Commander
Vice Admiral J P Kyd

ASSISTANT CHIEF OF NAVAL STAFF (POLICY)

2* Assistant Chief of Naval Staff (Policy)
Rear Admiral N W Hine

1* Head of Naval Staff
Commodore I S Lower

1* Head of RN Communications (Media Comms Hd)
Commodore G B Sutton OBE Rtd

1* Commander Regional Forces (CRF) & Naval Regional Commander Eastern England (NRC EE)
Commodore D G Elford

1* Naval Regional Commander Wales & Western England (NRC WWE)
Brigadier G W Fraser

1* Naval Regional Commander Northern England (NRC NE)
A/Commodore P Waterhouse

Naval Regional Commander Scotland & Northern Ireland (NRC SNI)
A/Captain C J Smith

COMMANDER UK MARITIME FORCES

2* Commander UK Maritime Forces (COMUKMARFOR)
Rear Admiral J P Kyd

1* Commander UK Task Group (COMATG)
Commodore A P Burns OBE

1* Commander Carrier Strike Group
Commodore A Betton OBE

COMMANDER UK AMPHIBIOUS FORCES
(COMMANDANT GENERAL ROYAL MARINES)

2* Commander UK Amphibious Forces & CGRM (COMUKAMPHIBFOR & CGRM)
Major General C R Stickland OBE

COMMANDER OPERATIONS

2* Commander Maritime Operations (COMOPS)
Rear Admiral P V Halton OBE

1* Commander 3 Commando Brigade RM (Comd 3CDO BDE RM)
Brigadier G Jenkins OBE

1* Commander Portsmouth Flotilla (COMPORFLOT)
Commodore C Wood

1* Commander Devonport Flotilla (COMDEVFLOT)
Commodore R J A Bellfield

1* Commander Faslane Flotilla (COMFASFLOT)
Commodore J L Perks OBE

ASSISTANT CHIEF NAVAL STAFF
(AVIATION, AMPHIBIOUS CAPABILITY & CARRIERS)

2* Assistant Chief of Naval Staff (Aviation, Amphibious Capability & Carriers) (ACNS(A&C))
& Rear Admiral Fleet Air Arm
Rear Admiral K E Blount CB OBE

1* Assistant Chief of Staff Carrier Strike & Aviation (ACOS CSAV)
Commodore S M Allen

1* Assistant Chief of Staff Land and Littoral Manoeuvre & Director Royal Marines (ACOS LLM)
Brigadier H J White

1* Commanding Officer RNAS Yeovilton (CO VL)
Commodore N H C Tindal

ASSISTANT CHIEF OF NAVAL STAFF (CAPABILITY)
& CHIEF OF STAFF NAVY COMMAND HQ

2* Assistant Chief of Naval Staff Capability (ACNS Cap)
Rear Admiral H D Beard

1* Assistant Chief of Staff Warfare (ACOS W)
Commodore M J Wainhouse

1* Assistant Chief of Staff Information Warfare (ACOS IW)
Commodore I G Annett

1* Assistant Chief of Staff Maritime Capability (ACOS Mar Cap)
Brigadier J A J Morris DSO

ASSISTANT CHIEF OF NAVAL STAFF (PERSONNEL),
NAVAL SECRETARY AND FLAG OFFICER RESERVES

2* Assistant Chief of Naval Staff (Personnel), Naval Secretary
and Flag Officer Reserves (NAVSEC/ACNS(Pers)/FORes)
Rear Admiral M A W Bath

1* Naval Assistant (NA)
Commodore R Murrison

1* Assistant Chief of Staff (People Capability)
Commodore M A W Bath

1* Assistant Chief of Staff Medical (ACOS MED)
Commodore I J Kennedy CBE QARRNS

1* Commander Maritime Reserves (COMMARRES)
Commodore M Quinn RNR

1* Head of Navy People Support
Angela Pope

DIRECTOR NAVAL SUPPORT

2* Director Naval Support (DNS)
Matthew S Harrison

1* Deputy Director Infrastructure
Matthew Allan

1* Assistant Chief of Staff Engineering Support (ACOS Eng Spt)
Commodore G T Little OBE

1* Assistant Chief of Staff Logistics & Infrastructure (ACOS Logs & Infra)
Commodore M T Clark

Commanding Officer HMNB Clyde (NBC(C))
Commodore D J M Doull ADC

Commanding Officer HMNB Devonport (NBC(D))
Commodore P Coulson ADC

Commanding Officer HMNB Portsmouth (NBC(P))
Commodore J G Higham ADC

ASSISTANT CHIEF OF NAVAL STAFF (SHIPS)

2* Assistant Chief of Naval Staff (Ships)
Rear Admiral C R S Gardner CBE

1* Assistant Chief of Staff Ships (ACOS Ships)
Commodore A Burns OBE

1* Assistant Chief of Staff Afloat Support (ACOS AFSUP)

Commodore D Lamb RFA

ASSISTANT CHIEF OF NAVAL STAFF (SUBMARINES) & FLAG OFFICER SCOTLAND & NORTHERN IRELAND

2* Assistant Chief of Naval Staff (Submarines) and Flag Officer Scotland & Northern Ireland
Rear Admiral J S Weale OBE

FLAG OFFICER SEA TRAINING & ASSISTANT CHIEF OF NAVAL STAFF (TRAINING)

2* Flag Officer Sea Training (FOST/ACNS T)
Rear Admiral W J Warrender CBE

1* Assistant Chief of Staff Training (ACOS T)
Commodore A Cree

1* Commander Operational Training (COM OT)
Commodore S P Huntington OBE

1* Commander Core Training (COMCORE)
Brigadier D L Kassapian

FINANCE DIRECTOR (NAVY)

2* Finance Director (Navy) (FD(N))
Colin M Evans

1* Deputy Finance Director (Navy)
John Hawthorne

1* Assistant Chief of Staff Resources & Plans (ACOS RP)
Commodore P J Hally

1* Command Secretary & Assistant Civilian Workforce Advisor (Comd Sec)
Deana Rouse

CHAPLAIN OF THE FLEET

2* Chaplain of the Fleet
The Venerable M J Gough QHC

Deputy Chaplain of the Fleet
The Reverend S Shackleton

OFFICERS ON THE ACTIVE LIST
OF THE ROYAL NAVY, THE ROYAL MARINES,
THE QUEEN ALEXANDRA'S
ROYAL NAVAL NURSING SERVICE
AND RETIRED AND EMERGENCY OFFICERS SERVING

Employee Name	Substantive Rank	Seniority Date	Branch	Specialisation	Organisation Name	Location Name
A						
Ablett, Eleanor L MBE	Cdre	28/08/2018	LOGS	L	ACOS	PORTSMOUTH
Ackland, Heber K MVO	Cdre	08/05/2018	LOGS	L	JFD	SWINDON
Adams, Andrew M.	Cdre	20/10/2014	ENG	MESM	SM DELIVERY AGENCY	BRISTOL
Albon, Ross CBE	R Adm	14/09/2018	LOGS	L BAR	JFD	LONDON
Allen, Stephen M	Cdre	01/08/2016	WAR	O SK6	FLEET CSAV	PORTSMOUTH
Annett, Ian G.	Cdre	24/07/2017	ENG	WE	FLEET CAP	PORTSMOUTH
Anstey, Robert J.	Cdre	17/04/2018	WAR	SM(CQ)	FOSNI	HELENSBURGH
Aplin, Adrian T MBE	Cdre	01/07/2014	LOGS	L	ACDS	BRISTOL
Asquith, Simon P OBE	Cdre	01/03/2018	WAR	SM(CQ)	JFD	NORTHWOOD
B						
Band, Sir Jonathon GCB DL	Adm	02/08/2002				
Bartlett, David S G OBE	Cdre	28/04/2016	ENG	AE	NAVY SAFETY CENTRE	PORTSMOUTH
Bath, Michael A W	R Adm	26/06/2018	LOGS	L SM	NAVSEC	PORTSMOUTH
Bathurst, Benjamin GCB DL	Adm of Fleet	10/07/1995				
Beard, Hugh D	R Adm	26/11/2018	WAR	SM(CQ)	ACNS	PORTSMOUTH
Beattie, Paul	Cdre	12/11/2018	WAR	AAWO	ACNS	PORTSMOUTH
Beckett, Keith A CBE	R Adm	04/11/2014	ENG	MESM		
Bellfield, Robert J A	Cdre	25/08/2017	WAR	PWO(U)	COMDEVFLOT	PLYMOUTH
Bennett, Paul CB OBE	V Adm	16/07/2018	WAR	PWO(A)	NATO ACT HQ SACT	NORFOLK
Betton, Andrew OBE	Cdre	01/12/2014	WAR	O LYNX	BDS	WASHINGTON
Bevis, Timothy J CBE	Maj Gen	31/05/2016	RM	GS	NATO BRUSSELS	BRUSSELS
Blount, Keith E CB OBE	R Adm	29/05/2015	WAR	P SK6	FLEET COS AVN	PORTSMOUTH
Bone, Darren N	Cdre	04/01/2015	WAR	PWO(A)	NATO BRUSSELS	BRUSSELS
Boyce, the Lord KG GCB OBE DL	Adm of Fleet	13/06/2014				
Briers, Matthew P	R Adm	02/01/2018	WAR	P SK4	D CEPP	LONDON
Burke, Paul D OBE	Cdre	09/01/2017	WAR	SM(CQ)	DG NUCLEAR	LONDON
Burns, Andrew P OBE	Cdre	03/05/2016	WAR	PWO(A)	SHIPS DIVISION	PORTSMOUTH
Burns, David I	Cdre	26/09/2018	WAR	PWO(C)	PJHQ	NORTHWOOD
C						
Cameron, Mark J OBE	Cdre	13/02/2018	ENG	WE	DEFENCE PEOPLE	LONDON
Carroll, Paul C	Cdre	16/10/2018	ENG	ME	DES COMSHIPS	BRISTOL
Childs, David G	Cdre	11/10/2016	ENG	AE P	DSA MAA	BRISTOL
Chivers, Paul A CBE	R Adm	08/12/2015	WAR	O LYNX	DSA MAA	BRISTOL
Clark, Matthew T	Cdre	12/06/2017	LOGS	L	FLEET SPT LOGS	PORTSMOUTH
Connell, Martin J	Cdre	10/02/2015	WAR	O LYNX	MTM FLEET HQ	PORTSMOUTH
Cooke-Priest, Nicholas C R OBE	Cdre	24/10/2018	WAR	O LYNX	HMS QUEEN ELIZABETH	
Copinger-Symes, Rory S CBE	Brig	25/07/2016	RM	HW	US COMMANDS	HAWAII
Coulson, Peter ADC	Cdre	07/12/2015	ENG	WE	NBD NBC HQ	HMS DRAKE
Cox, Rex J	Cdre	06/11/2018	WAR	AAWO	FMC CAPABILITY	LONDON
Cree, Andrew	Cdre	14/11/2016	ENG	TM	FLEET FOST	PORTSMOUTH

Employee Name	Substantive Rank	Seniority Date	Branch	Specialisation	Organisation Name	Location Name
D						
Dailey, Paul	Cdre	01/08/2016	ENG	WESM(SWS)	MTM RN GLOBAL	PAKISTAN
Dainton, Steven CBE	Cdre	02/06/2015	WAR	PWO(C)	UK MCC HQ	BAHRAIN
Doull, Donald J M	Cdre	19/06/2018	ENG	MESM	NBC CLYDE	HELENSBURGH
Duffy, Henry	Cdre	30/04/2017	WAR	PWO(C)	SERV ATTACHE/ADVISER	MUSCAT
E						
Entwisle, William N OBE MVO	R Adm	16/01/2017	WAR	P LYNX	CENTCOM SBMA	TAMPA
Essenhigh, Sir Nigel GCB DL	Adm	11/09/1998				
F						
Fraser, Timothy P CB	V Adm	26/06/2017	WAR	PWO(N)	PJHQ	NORTHWOOD
Fry, Jonathan M S	Cdre	21/01/2014	ENG	ME	DEFENCE PEOPLE	LONDON
G						
Gardner, Christopher R S CBE	R Adm	30/11/2015	LOGS	L SM	ACNS	PORTSMOUTH
Gough, Martyn	Chpln of the Fleet	31/07/2018	Ch S	Chaplain	CHPLN OF THE FLEET	PORTSMOUTH
Guy, Thomas J	Cdre	01/07/2018	WAR	PWO(U)	MOD NSD	NORFOLK
H						
Hally, Philip J MBE	Cdre	27/11/2017	LOGS	L CMA	FLEET ACOS(RP)	PORTSMOUTH
Halton, Paul V OBE	R Adm	24/10/2017	WAR	SM(CQ)	FLEET COMOPS	NORTHWOOD
Hatcher, Rhett S	Cdre	01/08/2016	WAR	P LYNX	OPS DIR	LONDON
Hayes, James V B	Cdre	30/07/2018	ENG	WESM(SWS)	SM DELIVERY AGENCY	BRISTOL
Henry, Timothy M OBE	Cdre	04/09/2018	WAR	PWO(U)	HQBF	GIBRALTAR
Higham, James G OBE ADC	Cdre	23/03/2015	ENG	WE	NBC PORTSMOUTH	PORTSMOUTH
Hine, Nicholas W CB	R Adm	01/09/2015	WAR	SM(CQ)	MOD CNS/ACNS	LONDON
Hodgson, Timothy C MBE	R Adm	01/07/2016	ENG	MESM	DG NUCLEAR	LONDON
Hollins, Rupert	Cdre	11/07/2016	LOGS	L BAR	MTM NELSON	PORTSMOUTH
Holmes, Matthew DSO	Maj Gen	07/05/2018	RM	GS	HQ RS	AFGHANISTAN
Hughes, Andrew S	Surg Cdre	25/07/2011	MED	GMP (C&S)	SG DMG	LICHFIELD
Huntington, Simon P OBE	Cdre	20/02/2017	WAR	PWO(U)	COM OT	PORTSMOUTH
J						
Jackson, Andrew S	Cdre	09/01/2018	ENG	MESM	DG NUCLEAR	LONDON
Jackson, Matthew J A DSO	Brig	11/12/2018	RM	GS	HQ 3 CDO BDE RM	PLYMOUTH
Jenkins, Gwyn OBE	Brig	01/07/2015	RM	GS	NCHQ	PORTSMOUTH
Johnstone, Clive C C KBE CB	V Adm	13/10/2015	WAR	PWO(A)	NATO ACO MARITIME COMMAND HQ	NORTHWOOD
Jones, Philip A KCB	Adm	08/04/2016	WAR	PWO(C)	MOD CNS/ACNS	LONDON
K						
Kassapian, David L	Brig	22/03/2016	RM	GS	NAVY CORE TRG HQ	PLYMOUTH
Kennedy, Inga J CBE	Cdre	09/02/2015	QARNNS	Nurse Officer	NCHQ MEDDIV	PORTSMOUTH
Key, Benjamin J CBE	V Adm	10/02/2016	WAR	O LYNX	FLEET COMMANDER	PORTSMOUTH
Kingwell, John M L CBE	R Adm	14/10/2013	WAR	PWO(U)	JFD	LONDON
Kyd, Jeremy P	R Adm	28/10/2018	WAR	PWO(N)	UKMARBATSTAFF	PORTSMOUTH
Kyte, Andrew J	R Adm	19/11/2018	LOGS	L	ACDS	LONDON
L						
Lines, James M	Cdre	06/05/2014	LOGS	L	MTM MOD CNS/ACNS	LONDON
Lister, Simon R KCB OBE	V Adm	27/11/2013	ENG	MESM	MTM NELSON	PORTSMOUTH
Little, Graeme T OBE	Cdre	17/07/2012	ENG	ME	ACOS	PORTSMOUTH
Long, Adrian M	Cdre	01/07/2015	ENG	WE	MTM NELSON	PORTSMOUTH
Lovegrove, Raymond A	Cdre	30/04/2018	ENG	WE	DIO SAPT	ANDOVER
Lowe, Timothy M CBE	R Adm	17/09/2012	WAR	PWO(N) PWO(U)	LOAN HYDROG	TAUNTON
Lower, Iain S	Cdre	01/08/2016	WAR	AAWO	MOD NSD	LONDON
M						
Macdonald, John R	Cdre	22/07/2013	ENG	WESM(TWS)	SM DELIVERY AGENCY	BRISTOL
Macleod, James N	Cdre	14/11/2014	ENG	WE	DEFENCE PEOPLE	LONDON
Magowan, Robert A CB CBE	Maj Gen	03/06/2016	RM	GS	ACDS	LONDON
Manson, Thomas E OBE	Cdre	08/08/2016	ENG	AE P	DES COMAIR	BRISTOL
Marshall, Paul CBE	Cdre	20/03/2017	ENG	ME	NAVY SHIPS ACQ PMO	PORTSMOUTH
Matthews, David W	Cdre	22/02/2018	ENG	WESM(TWS)	SM DELIVERY AGENCY	BRISTOL

Employee Name	Substantive Rank	Seniority Date	Branch	Specialisation	Organisation Name	Location Name
Maybery, James E	Brig	01/02/2018	RM	GS	NCHQ	PORTSMOUTH
Messenger, Gordon K KCB DSO* OBE ADC	Gen	16/05/2016	RM	MLDR	VCDS	LONDON
Methven, Paul CB	R Adm	05/01/2017	ENG	MESM	SM DELIVERY AGENCY	BRISTOL
Middleton, Christopher S MBE	Brig	26/11/2018	RM	LC	JFIG	HUNTINGDON
Millar, Stuart W S	Surg Cdre	31/07/2017	MED	GMP (C&S)	SG MED	LONDON
Moorhouse, Stephen OBE	Cdre	11/09/2018	WAR	O SKW	HMS PRINCE OF WALES	
Morley, James D	R Adm	09/04/2018	WAR	PWO(A)	JFC	NORTHWOOD
Morris, James A J DSO	Brig	01/07/2015	RM	GS	FLEET CAP	PORTSMOUTH
Morritt, Dain C	Cdre	25/08/2015	ENG	WE	MTM FLEET HQ	PORTSMOUTH
Murchison, Ewen A DSO MBE	Brig	30/11/2017	RM	GS	JFD	SWINDON
Murrison, Richard A	Cdre	03/08/2015	LOGS	L	NAVSEC	PORTSMOUTH

P

Parkin, James M B	Cdre	22/05/2018	WAR	PWO FC	COMATG	PLYMOUTH
Pearson, Stephen	Cdre	15/02/2016	WAR	O SKW	DSA DMR	BRISTOL
Pentreath, Jonathan P OBE	R Adm	04/04/2017	WAR	P SK4	HQ JHC	ANDOVER
Perks, James L OBE	Cdre	01/07/2018	WAR	SM(CQ)	COMFASFLOT	HELENSBURGH
Pierson, Matthew F	Brig	24/07/2017	RM	GS	NATO BRUSSELS	BRUSSELS

Q

Quinn, Martin	Cdre	19/04/2016	WAR	MEDIA OPS (RES)	FLEET CMR	PORTSMOUTH

R

Radakin, Antony D CB	V Adm	27/03/2018	WAR	PWO(U)	2SL	PORTSMOUTH
Robinson, Guy A OBE	R Adm	13/11/2017	WAR	PWO(A)	STRIKFORNATO	LISBON
Robinson, Michael P	Cdre	01/07/2014	ENG	MESM	SM DELIVERY AGENCY	BRISTOL

S

Scott, Simon J OBE	Brig	06/11/2018	RM	LC	1 AGRM	PLYMOUTH
Shackleton, Scott	RN Prncpl Chpln	21/08/2017	Ch S	Chaplain	CHPLN OF THE FLEET	PORTSMOUTH
Slater, Sir Jock GCB LVO DL	Adm	29/01/1991				
Sparkes, Peter J	Cdre	01/06/2015	WAR	PWO(C)	CDSLO	WASHINGTON DC
Stanhope, Sir Mark GCB OBE DL	Adm	10/07/2004				
Stickland, Charles R OBE	Maj Gen	23/10/2017	RM	LC	COMUKAMPHIBFOR	PORTSMOUTH

T

Taylor, Peter G D OBE	Brig	06/05/2014	RM	GS	CABINET OFFICE	LONDON
Thompson, Richard C CBE	R Adm	27/09/2016	ENG	AE	DES COMAIR	DEESIDE
Tindal, Nicolas H C	Cdre	18/04/2017	WAR	P SK6	RNAS YEOVILTON	YEOVIL
Toy, Malcolm J	R Adm	03/07/2018	ENG	AE	DSA MAA	BRISTOL

U

Urry, Simon R MBE	Brig	04/12/2017	RM	GS	NCHQ	PORTSMOUTH
Utley, Michael K OBE	Cdre	01/10/2018	WAR	PWO(A)	CARRIER STRIKE GP	PORTSMOUTH

W

Wainhouse, Michael J	Cdre	22/04/2014	WAR	PWO(A)	FLEET CAP	PORTSMOUTH
Walker, Alasdair J CB OBE QHS	Surg V Adm	17/12/2015	MED	GS (C&S)	MTM NELSON	LICHFIELD
Walliker, Michael J D CBE	Cdre	12/06/2014	WAR	SM(CQ)	JFD	SWINDON
Warrender, William J CBE	R Adm	12/06/2018	WAR	PWO(A)	FOST	PLYMOUTH
Warwick, Philip D	Cdre	17/03/2015	WAR	PWO(U)	MTM NORTHWOOD	NORTHWOOD
Washer, Nicholas B J	Cdre	03/12/2018	WAR	PWO(C)	PJHQ	NORTHWOOD
Weale, John S CB OBE	R Adm	18/05/2015	WAR	SM(CQ)	FOSNI	HELENSBURGH
West, the Lord GCB DSC PC	Adm	30/11/2000				
White, Haydn J ADC	Brig	05/09/2017	RM	LC	FLEET CAP	PORTSMOUTH
Williams, Martyn J	Cdre	05/12/2017	ENG	WESM(TWS)	DES COMSHIPS	BRISTOL
Winter, Richard J	Cdre	30/04/2018	ENG	WE	ISS OPS	CORSHAM
Wood, Craig	Cdre	12/12/2017	WAR	PWO(A)	COMPORFLOT	PORTSMOUTH
Wood, Robert	Cdre	29/05/2018	LOGS	L BAR	NCHQ CNLS	PORTSMOUTH
Woods, Timothy C	Cdre	01/05/2018	ENG	TM(SM)	DALSC	SWINDON

Z

Zambellas, Sir George GCB DSC DL	Adm	06/01/2012				

SENIORITY LIST

ADMIRALS OF THE FLEET

Edinburgh, His Royal Highness The Prince Philip, Duke of, KG, KT, OM, GBE, AC, QSO ......15 Jan 53
Bathurst, Sir (David) Benjamin, GCB, DL ....10 Jul 95
Wales, His Royal Highness The Prince Charles, Prince of, KG, KT, CGB, OM, AK, QSO, PC, ADC ...16 Jun 12
Boyce, the Lord, KG, GCB, OBE, DL.. 13-Jun-14

ADMIRALS

FORMER CHIEF OF DEFENCE STAFF, FIRST SEA LORD OR VICE CHIEF OF DEFENCE STAFF WHO REMAIN ON THE ACTIVE LIST

Slater, Sir Jock (John Cunningham Kirkwood), GCB, LVO, DL ....29 Jan 91
Essenhigh, Sir Nigel, GCB, DL.. 11 Sep 98
West, the Lord, GCB, DSC, PC ....30 Nov 00
Band, Sir Jonathon, GCB, DL... 2 Aug 02
Stanhope, Sir Mark, GCB, OBE, DL...10 Jul 04
Zambellas, Sir George, GCB, DSC, DL... 06-Jan-12

ADMIRAL

Jones, Sir Philip, KCB, ADC 08-Apr-16
(CHIEF OF NAVAL STAFF AND FIRST SEA LORD)

VICE ADMIRALS

Johnstone, Clive Charles Carrutherslowe KBE CB 13-Oct-15
(COMMANDER MARITIME COMMAND)

Key, Benjamin John, CBE 10-Feb-16
(FLEET COMMANDER and CHIEF NAVAL WARFARE OFFICER)

Fraser, Timothy Peter, CB.. 26-Jun-17
(CHIEF OF JOINT OPERATIONS)

Radakin, Anthony David, CB 27-Mar-18
(SECOND SEA LORD AND DEPUTY CHIEF OF NAVAL STAFF)

Bennett, Paul, CB OBE 16-Jul-18
(CHIEF OF STAFF TO THE SUPREME ALLIED COMMANDER (TRANSFORMATION))

REAR ADMIRALS

Weale, John Stewart, CB OBE 18-May-15
(FLAG OFFICER SCOTLAND & NORTHERN IRELAND & ASSISTANT CHIEF OF NAVAL STAFF (SUBMARINES) and REAR ADMIRAL SUBMARINES)

Blount, Keith Edward, CB, OBE 29-May-15
(ASSISTANT CHIEF OF NAVAL STAFF (AVIATION & CARRIERS) and REAR ADMIRAL FLEET AIR ARM)

Hine, Nicholas William, CB 01-Sep-15
(ASSISTANT CHIEF OF NAVAL STAFF (POLICY))

Gardner, Christopher Reginald Summers, CBE 30-Nov-15
(ASSISTANT CHIEF OF NAVAL STAFF (SHIPS) and CHIEF NAVAL LOGISTICS OFFICER)

Kingwell, John Matthew Leonard, CBE..03-May-16
(DEPUTY COMMANDANT ROYAL COLLEGE OF DEFENCE STUDIES)

Hodgson, Timothy Charles, MBE 01-Jul-16
(DIRECTOR SUBMARINE CAPABILITY)

Methven, Paul CB 05-Jan-17
(DIRECTOR SUBMARINES ACQUISITION)

Entwisle, William Nicholas, OBE, MVO 17-Jan-17
(SENIOR BRITISH MILITARY ADVISER CENTRAL COMMAND)

Pentreath, Jonathan Patrick, OBE 04-Apr-17
(COMMANDANT JOINT HELICOPTER COMMAND)

Halton, Paul Vincent, OBE... 31-Oct-17
(COMMANDER OPERATIONS)

Robinson, Guy Antony, OBE... 13-Nov-17
(DEPUTY COMMANDER NAVAL STRIKING & SUPPORT FORCES NATO)

Briers, Matt... 12-Jan-18
(DIRECTOR CARRIER STRIKE)

Morley, James..09-Apr-18
(DIRECTOR CAPABILITY JOINT FORCES COMMAND) ....

Warrender, William John, CBE 12-Jun-18
(FLAG OFFICER SEA TRAINING)

Bath, Michael Anthony William.. 26-Jun-18
(ASSISTANT CHIEF OF NAVAL STAFF (PERSONNEL), NAVAL SECRETARY & FLAG OFFICER RESERVES)

Beckett, Keith Andrew, CBE... 01-Jul-18
(CHIEF STRATEGIC SYSTEMS EXECUTIVE)

Toy, Malcolm John... 03-Jul-18
(TECHNICAL DIRECTOR MILITARY AVIATION AUTHORITY)

Lowe, Timothy Miles, CBE..12-Sep-18
(UK HYDROGRAPHIC OFFICE ACTING CHIEF EXECUTIVE AND ACCOUNTING OFFICER)

Albon, Ross CBE 14-Sep-18
(SENIOR DIRECTING STAFF, ROYAL COLLEGE OF DEFENCE STUDIES

Kyd, Jeremy Paul..28-Oct-18
(COMMANDER UK MARITIME FORCES and REAR ADMIRAL SURFACE SHIPS)

Beard, Hugh 26-Nov-18
(ASSISTANT CHIEF OF NAVAL STAFF(CAPABILITY))

Kyte, Andrew... 19-Nov-18
(ASSISTANT CHIEF OF DEFENCE STAFF (LOGISTIC OPERATIONS)).................................

Appointed but not yet in post by 1 Jan 19

Major General desig G Jenkins OBE
(ASSISTANT CHIEF OF NAVAL STAFF (POLICY)) in Jan 19

Rear Admiral desig M J Connell...
(ASSISTANT CHIEF OF NAVAL STAFF (AVIATION & CAPABILITY) in Feb 19

Rear Admiral desig J N Macleod (Jim) ....
DEFENCE SERVICES SECRETARY in Apr 19

Major General desig J A J Morris DSO ....
DIRECTOR JOINT WARFARE in Apr 19

In the Margin

Lister, Sir Simon Robert, KCB, OBE 27-Nov-13
Chivers, Paul, CBE...08-Dec-15
Walker, Alasdair James, CB OBE QHS...17-Dec-15
Thompson, Richard Andrew CBE...27-Sep-16

Since the publication of the last Navy Directory, the following officers have joined, or will be joining, the Retired List:

Vice Admiral Sir Jonathan Woodcock KCB OBE 30 Jun 18
Vice Admiral D L Potts CB 13 Oct 18
Rear Admiral A J Burton 2 Feb 18
Rear Admiral P A McAlpine CBE 7 Apr 18
Rear Admiral R K Tarrant CB 11 Apr 18
Rear Admiral R Stokes CBE 5 May 18
Rear Admiral G A Mackay CBE 15 May 18
Rear Admiral S P Hardern 1 Sep 18
Rear Admiral J R H Clink CBE 19 Sep 18
Rear Admiral S P Williams CB CVO 16 Oct 18
The Venerable I J Wheatley CB 16 Nov 18

COMMODORES

2012

Little, Graeme T OBE.............................. 17/07/2012

2013

Macdonald, John R 22/07/2013

2014

Fry, Jonathan M S 21/01/2014
Wainhouse, Michael J 22/04/2014
Lines, James M...................................... 06/05/2014
Walliker, Michael J D CBE 12/06/2014
Aplin, Adrian T MBE............................. 01/07/2014
Robinson, Michael P.............................. 01/07/2014
Adams, Andrew M................................. 20/10/2014
Macleod, James N.................................. 14/11/2014
Betton, Andrew OBE............................ 01/12/2014

2015

Bone, Darren N...................................... 04/01/2015
Kennedy, Inga J CBE 09/02/2015
Connell, Martin J 10/02/2015
Warwick, Philip D.................................. 17/03/2015
Higham, James G OBE ADC 23/03/2015
Sparkes, Peter J 01/06/2015
Dainton, Steven CBE............................ 02/06/2015
Long, Adrian M 01/07/2015
Murrison, Richard A............................... 03/08/2015

Morritt, Dain C 25/08/2015
Coulson, Peter ADC 07/12/2015

2016

Pearson, Stephen................................... 15/02/2016
Quinn, Martin 19/04/2016
Bartlett, David S G OBE........................ 28/04/2016
Burns, Andrew P OBE........................... 03/05/2016
Hollins, Rupert 11/07/2016
Allen, Stephen M................................... 01/08/2016
Dailey, Paul 01/08/2016
Hatcher, Rhett S.................................... 01/08/2016
Lower, Iain S... 01/08/2016
Manson, Thomas E OBE......................... 08/08/2016
Childs, David G...................................... 11/10/2016
Cree, Andrew 14/11/2016

2017

Burke, Paul D OBE................................ 09/01/2017
Huntington, Simon P OBE 20/02/2017
Marshall, Paul CBE............................... 20/03/2017
Tindal, Nicolas H C 18/04/2017
Duffy, Henry 30/04/2017
Clark, Matthew T.................................. 12/06/2017
Annett, Iain G....................................... 24/07/2017
Bellfield, Robert J A............................... 25/08/2017
Hally, Philip J MBE................................ 27/11/2017
Williams, Martyn J................................ 05/12/2017

Wood, Craig.. 12/12/2017

2018

Jackson, Andrew S................................. 09/01/2018
Cameron, Mark J OBE........................... 13/02/2018
Matthews, David W 22/02/2018
Asquith, Simon P OBE 01/03/2018
Anstey, Robert J.................................... 17/04/2018
Lovegrove, Raymond A 30/04/2018
Winter, Richard J................................... 30/04/2018
Woods, Timothy C 01/05/2018
Ackland, Heber K MVO......................... 08/05/2018
Parkin, James M B................................. 22/05/2018
Wood, Robert.. 29/05/2018
Doull, Donald J M 19/06/2018
Guy, Thomas J 01/07/2018
Perks, James L OBE 01/07/2018
Hayes, James V B 30/07/2018
Ablett, Eleanor L MBE 28/08/2018
Henry, Timothy M OBE......................... 04/09/2018
Moorhouse, Stephen OBE 11/09/2018
Burns, David I....................................... 26/09/2018
Utley, Michael K OBE 01/10/2018
Carroll, Paul C 16/10/2018
Cooke-Priest, Nicholas C R OBE............. 24/10/2018
Cox, Rex J 06/11/2018
Beattie, Paul... 12/11/2018
Washer, Nicholas B J 03/12/2018

MEDICAL OFFICERS

SURGEON VICE ADMIRALS

2015

Walker, Alasdair J CB OBE QHS............ 17/12/2015

SURGEON COMMODORES

2011

Hughes, Andrew S............................. 25/07/2011

2017

Millar, Stuart W S................................ 31/07/2017

QUEEN ALEXANDRA'S ROYAL NAVAL NURSING SERVICE

COMMODORE

2015

Kennedy, Inga J CBE 09/02/2015

CHAPLAINS

CHAPLAIN OF THE FLEET & PRINCIPAL ANGLICAN CHAPLAIN

The Venerable Martyn Gough, QHC...Tuesday, 31 July 2018
Chaplain of the Fleet and Archdeacon for the Royal Navy

DEPUTY CHAPLAIN OF THE FLEET

The Reverend Professor Scott Shackleton .... Monday, 21 August 2017

ROYAL MARINES

CAPTAIN GENERAL

His Royal Highness Prince Henry of Wales KCVO

HONORARY COLONEL

His Majesty King Harald V of Norway, KG, GCVO

COLONELS COMMANDANT

Major General David Wilson, CB, CBE 01-May-12
(Colonel Commandant Royal Marines)

Major General J S Mason MBE ....Dec 18
(Representative Colonel Commandant Royal Marines)

GENERAL

Messenger, Sir Gordon, KCB, DSO*, OBE, ADC 16-May-16
(VICE CHIEF OF DEFENCE STAFF MAY 16)

MAJOR GENERALS

Bevis, Timothy James, CBE 31-May-16
(DIRECTOP OPERATIONS & PLANS, INTERNATIONAL MILITARY STAFF MAY 16)

Magowan, Robert Andrew, CBE 10-Dec-18
(ASSISTANT CHIEF OF DEFENCE STAFF STAFF (CAPABILITY & FORCE DESIGN) DEC 18)

Stickland, Charles Richard, OBE.. 8-Nov-17
(COMMANDER UK AMPHIBIOUS FORCES NOV 17 & COMMANDANT GENERAL ROYAL MARINES JAN 18)

Holmes, MJ Holmes, DSO...7 May 18
DEPUTY ADVISOR MINISTRY OF THE INTERIOR

BRIGADIERS

2014

Taylor, Peter G D OBE 06/05/2014

2015

Jenkins, Gwyn OBE 01/07/2015

Morris, James A J DSO 01/07/2015

2016

Kassapian, David L 22/03/2016

Copinger-Symes, Rory S CBE................. 25/07/2016

2017

Pierson, Matthew F 24/07/2017

White, Haydn J ADC 05/09/2017

Murchison, Ewen A DSO MBE.............. 30/11/2017

Urry, Simon R MBE............................... 04/12/2017

2018

Maybery, James E 01/02/2018

Scott, Simon J OBE............................... 06/11/2018

Middleton, Christopher S MBE............. 26/11/2018

Jackson, Matthew J A DSO 11/12/2018

RFA OFFICERS

HONORARY COMMODORE

His Royal Highness Prince Edward, The Earl of Wessex, KG, KCVO, ADC

COMMODORE

Lamb, Duncan

COMMODORE (Engineers)

Ian Schumaker (retiring 11 June 2019)

SHIPS OF THE ROYAL FLEET AUXILIARY SERVICE

ARGUS, Aviation Training Ship
BFPO 433

CARDIGAN BAY, Bay Class Landing Ship
BFPO 436

FORT AUSTIN, Fleet Replenishment Ship
BFPO 439

FORT ROSALIE, Fleet Replenishment Ship
BFPO 441

FORT VICTORIA, Fleet Replenishment Ship
BFPO 442

LYME BAY, Bay Class Landing Ship
BFPO 447

MOUNTS BAY, Bay Class Landing Ship
BFPO 448

TIDESPRING, Fleet Tanker
BFPO 457

WAVE RULER, Fast Fleet Tanker
BFPO 431

WAVE KNIGHT, Fast Fleet Tanker
BFPO 432

OFFICERS PRACTISING AS NAVAL BARRISTERS

ROYAL NAVY

COMMODORE
Wood, Rob

HONORARY OFFICERS IN THE MARITIME RESERVES

ROYAL NAVAL RESERVE

Vice Admiral HRH Prince Michael of Kent GCVO
Vice Admiral Sir Donald Gosling KCVO
Vice Admiral The Right Honourable The Lord Sterling of Plaistow GCVO CBE
Captain Sir Eric Dancer KCVO CBE JP
Captain Sir Michael Hintze
Captain Carl Richardson
Captain The Earl of Dalhousie
Captain Jan Kopernicki CMG
Captain Adam Gosling
Captain Dame Mary Peters DBE
Captain Stephen Watson
Captain Christopher Wells
Captain Jeremy Greaves
Captain Sir Robin Knox-Johnston CBE RD*
Captain The Lord Hennessy of Nympsfield FBA
Captain Alderman The Right Honourable The Lord Mountevans
Commander Peter Moore RD* DL
Commander Dee Caffari MBE
Commander Anthony Lima MBE RD*
Commander Simon Bird
Commander Dan Snow
Commander Sarah Kenny
Commander The Earl of Derby DL
Commander Lance Batchelor
Commander Mark Fox JP
Commander James Sproule
Lieutenant Commander Tracey Curtis-Taylor
Lieutenant Commander Durdana Ansari
Lieutenant Commander Raj Aggarwal
Lieutenant Commander Keith Knowles
Lieutenant Commander Philip Braat
Chaplain The Reverend Canon David Parrott
Chaplain The Reverend Neil Gardner

HONORARY OFFICERS IN THE MARITIME RESERVES

ROYAL MARINES RESERVE

Colonel Phil Loynes
Colonel David Watt
Lieutenant Colonel David Gosling
Lieutenant Colonel Bear Grylls

OFFICERS OF THE ACTIVE LIST OF THE ROYAL NAVAL RESERVE

Name	Rank	Seniority	Branch	Unit
B				
BECKETT, KEITH A	R Adm	04-Nov-14	ENG	SM DELIVERY AGENCY
Q				
QUINN, MARTIN	Cdre	19-Apr-16	WAR	FLEET CMR
R				
REYNOLDS, NELSON OBE	Cdre	05-Nov-03	WAR	HMS HIBERNIA
S				
STEVENSON, CHARLES B H	Cdre	03-Nov-08	WAR	FOSNNI
T				
THORNE, STEPHEN	Cdre	25-Jan-07	WAR	HMS KING ALFRED

SPARE

YACHT CLUBS USING A SPECIAL ENSIGN

Yachts belonging to members of the following Yacht Clubs may, subject to certain conditions, obtain a Warrant to wear a Special Ensign.

Club	Address (where applicable)

WHITE ENSIGN

Royal Yacht Squadron	Royal Yacht Squadron, The Castle, Cowes, Isle of Wight. PO31 7QT

BLUE ENSIGN

Hornet Services Sailing Club	Haslar Road, Gosport, Hants. PO12 2AQ
Royal Naval Club and Royal Albert Yacht Club	17 Pembroke Road, Portsmouth. PO1 2NT
Royal Brighton Yacht Club	253 The Esplanade, Middle Brighton, Victoria 3186, Australia
Royal Cinque Ports Yacht Club	5 Waterloo Crescent, Dover. CT16 1LA
Royal Cruising Club	C/O Royal Thames Yacht Club, 60 Knightsbridge, London. SW1X 7LF
Royal Dorset Yacht Club	11 Custom House Quay, Weymouth. DT4 8BG
Royal Engineer Yacht Club	BATCIS DT, Yew 0 1039, MOD Abbeywood, Bristol. BS36 8JH
Royal Geelong Yacht Club	25 Eastern Beach Road, Geelong, 3220 Victoria, Australia. Email: INFO@RGYC.com.au
Royal Gourock Yacht Club	Ashton, Gourock. PA19 1DA
Royal Highland Yacht Club	Achavraid, Clachan, Tarbert. PA29 6XN
Royal Marines Sailing Club	10 Haslar Marina, Haslar Road, Gosport. PO12 1NU
Royal Melbourne Yacht Squadron	Pier Road, St Kilda, 3182 Victoria, Australia.
Royal Motor Yacht Club	Panorama Road, Sandbanks, Poole. BH13 7RN
Royal Naval Sailing Association	10 Haslar Marina, Haslar Road, Gosport. PO12 1NU
Royal Naval Volunteer Reserve Yacht Club	The Naval Club, 38 Hill Street, Mayfair, London. W1X 8DB
Royal New Zealand Yacht Squadron	P.O. Box 46 182, Herne Bay, Auckland 1147, New Zealand.
Royal Northern and Clyde Yacht Club	Rhu, By Helensburgh. G84 8NG
Royal Perth Yacht Club of Western Australia	Australia II Drive, Crawley, Western Australia, Australia.

Royal Port Nicholson Yacht Club .... 103 Oriental Parade, Oriental Bay,
6011 New Zealand.

Royal Queensland Yacht Squadron................................. 578 Royal Esplanade, Manly,
4179 Queensland.

Royal Scottish Motor Yacht Club.................................... 35 Brueacre Drive, Wemyss Bay. PA18 6HA

Royal Solent Yacht Club... The Square, Yarmouth,
Isle of Wight. PO41 0NS

Royal South Australian Yacht Squadron .... 161 Oliver Rogers Road, Outer Harbour,
5018 South Australia, Australia.
Email: member.services@RSAYS.com.au

Royal Southern Yacht Club .... Rope Walk, Hamble, Southampton. SO31 4HB

Royal Sydney Yacht Squadron .... P.O. Box 484, Milson's Point,
New South Wales. 1565

Royal Temple Yacht Club .... 6 Westcliff Mansions, Ramsgate. CT11 9HY

Royal Thames Yacht Club... 60 Knightsbridge, London. SW1X 7LF

Royal Victorian Motor Yacht Club .... 260 Nelson Place, Williamstown, Victoria
3016, Australia.
Email: Admin@RVMYC.com.au

Royal Western Yacht Club of England .... Queen Anne's Battery, Plymouth. PL4 0TW

Royal Western Yacht Club of Scotland .... Shandon, Helensburgh. G84 8NP

Royal Yacht Club of Tasmania.. Marieville Esplanade, Sandy Bay, Tasmania
7005, Australia.
Email: RYCT@RYCT.org.au

Royal Yacht Club of Victoria... 120 Nelson Place, Williamstown, Victoria
3016, Australia.

Sussex Motor Yacht Club .... 85-89 Brighton Road, Shoreham by Sea.
BN43 6RE

BLUE ENSIGN DEFACED BY BADGE OF CLUB

Aldeburgh Yacht Club .... Slaughden Road, Aldeburgh. IP15 5NA

Army Sailing Association .... Clayton Barracks, Thornhill Road, Aldershot.
GU11 2BG

Bar Yacht Club... 47 Tower Bridge Wharf, 86 St Katharine's
Way, London. E1W 1UR

City Livery Yacht Club .... 79 Palace Gardens Terrace, London. W8 4EE

Conway Club Cruising Association................................. Honorary Treasurer, Lt Cdr Sewell RNR,
87 Roxeth Hill, Harrow, Middlesex.

Cruising Yacht Club of Australia .... New Beach Road, Darling Point,
New South Wales 2027, Australia.

Household Division Yacht Club ....RHQ Scots Guards, Wellington Barracks, Birdcage Walk, London. SW1E 6HQ

Little Ship Club ....Bell Wharf Lane, Upper Thames Street, London. EC4R 3TB

Little Ship Club (Queensland Squadron) ....PO Box 10, Dunwich, 4183 Queensland, Australia.

Medway Cruising Club...Anchorage Yard, Waterside Lane, Gillingham. ME7 2SE

Old Worcesters Yacht Club ....21 Brunel Quays, Lostwithiel. PL22 0JB

Parkstone Yacht Club..Pearce Avenue, Parkstone, Poole. BH14 8EH

Rochester Cruising Yacht Club ....10 The Esplanade, Rochester. ME1 1QN

Royal Air Force Yacht Club...Riverside House, Rope Walk, Hamble, Southampton. SO31 4HD

Royal Akarana Yacht Club...P.O. Box 42-004, Orakei, Auckland, New Zealand.

Royal Anglesey Yacht Club...6-7 Green Edge, Beaumaris. LL58 8BY

Royal Armoured Corps Yacht Club.................................Kings Royal Hussars, Aliwall Barracks, Tidworth. SP9 7BB

Royal Artillery Yacht Club...Fort Blockhouse, Haslar Road, Gosport. PO12 2AB

Royal Australian Navy Sailing Association ....1C New Beach Road, Sir David Martin Reserve, Rushcutters Bay, NSW 2027, Australia.

Royal Bermuda Yacht Club...P.O. Box 894, Hamilton HM DX, Bermuda.

Royal Bombay Yacht Club ....Chhatrapati Shivaji Maharaj Marg, Apollo Bunder, Mumbai, 400 001, India.

Royal Burnham Yacht Club ....The Quay, Burnham-on-Crouch. CM0 8AU

Royal Channel Islands Yacht Club ....Le Mont du Boulevard, St Brelade, Jersey. JE3 8AD

Royal Corinthian Yacht Club ....The Quay, Burnham-on-Crouch. CM0 8AX

Royal Cornwall Yacht Club..Greenbank, Falmouth. TR11 2SP

Royal Dee Yacht Club ....Siglen, Pulford, Chester. CH4 9EL

Royal Forth Yacht Club ....Middle Pier, Granton Harbour, Edinburgh. EH5 1HF

Royal Freshwater Bay Yacht Club of Western Australia...PO Box 373, Cottesloe 6911, Western Australia, Australia.

Royal Gibraltar Yacht Club..26 Queensway, Gibraltar. Email: RGYC@Gibraltar.GI

Royal Hamilton Yacht Club ....Foot of McNab Street North, Hamilton, Ontario, Canada. Email: Sail@RHYC.ca

Royal Harwich Yacht Club..Wolverstone, Ipswich. IP9 1AT

Royal Hong Kong Yacht Club...Kellett Island, Causeway Bay, Hong Kong.

Royal Irish Yacht Club ....Harbour Road, Dun Laoghaire,
County Dublin, Eire.

Royal Jamaica Yacht Club ....Norman Manly International Airport,
Palisadoes Park, Kingston, Jamaica.
Email: RJYC@Flowja.com

Royal London Yacht Club...The Parade, Cowes, Isle of Wight PO31 7QS

Royal Malta Yacht Club...Hon. Secretary, Royal Yacht Club, TA'XBIEX
Seafront, XBX 1028, Malta.

Royal Mersey Yacht Club ....Bedford Road East, Rock Ferry,
Birkenhead. CH42 1LS

Royal Motor Yacht Club of New South Wales ....Wunulla Road, Point Piper 2027,
New South Wales, Australia.

Royal Nassau Sailing Club ....P.O. Box SS 6891, Nassau, Bahamas.

Royal Natal Yacht Club ....Yacht Mole, Durban Harbour, Kwa Zulu Natal,
South Africa.

Royal North of Ireland Yacht Club ....7 Seafront Road, Holywood,
County Down. BT18 OBB

Royal Northumberland Yacht Club ....South Harbour, Blyth. NE24 3PB

Royal Ocean Racing Club ....20 St James' Place, London. SW1A 1NN

Royal Plymouth Corinthian Yacht Club...........................Madeira Road, The Barbican,
Plymouth. PL1 2NY

Royal Prince Alfred Yacht Club.......................................16 Mitala Street, Newport 2106, NSW,
Australia.

Royal Prince Edward Yacht Club.....................................P.O. Box 2502 Bondi Junction, New South
Wales 1355, Australia.
Email: Mail@rpeyc.co.au

Royal Southampton Yacht Club ....1 Channel Way, Ocean Village,
Southampton. SO14 3QF

Royal Suva Yacht Club ....P.O. Box 335 Suva, Republic of Fiji.
Email: RSYC@kidanet.net.fj

Royal Torbay Yacht Club ....12 Beacon Terrace, Torquay. TQ1 2BH

Royal Ulster Yacht Club...101 Clifton Road, Bangor, County Down.
BT20 5HY

Royal Welsh Yacht Club ....Porth Yr Aur Caernarfon. LL55 1SN

Royal Yorkshire Yacht Club...1-3 Windsor Crescent, Bridlington. YO15 3HX

Severn Motor Yacht Club...Bath Road, Broomhall, Worcester. WR5 3HR

Sussex Yacht Club..85-89 Brighton Road, Shoreham-by-Sea
BN43 6RE

Thames Motor Yacht Club ....The Green, Hampton Court, Surrey. KT8 9BW

The Cruising Association ....CA House, 1 Northey Street, Limehouse Basin, London. E14 8BT

The House of Lords Yacht Club ....Overseas Office, House of Lords, London. SW1A 0PW

The Medway Yacht Club................................Lower Upnor, Rochester. ME2 4XB

The Poole Harbour Yacht Club ....40 Salterns Way, Poole, Dorset. BH14 8JR

The Poole Yacht Club.......................................The Yacht Haven, New Harbour Road West, Hamworthy, Poole. BH15 4AQ

RED ENSIGN DEFACED BY BADGE OF CLUB

Brixham Yacht Club ....Overgang, Brixham. TQ5 8AR

House of Commons Yacht Club ....C/O RYA, RYA House, Ensign Way, Hamble, Southampton. SO31 4YA

Lloyd's Yacht Club ....-

Royal Dart Yacht Club....................................Priory Street, Kingswear, Dartmouth. TQ6 0AB

Royal Fowey Yacht Club..................................Whitford Yard, Fowey. PL23 1BH

Royal Hamilton Amateur Dinghy Club ....25 Pomander Road, Hamilton, PG05, Bermuda.

Royal Lymington Yacht Club ....Bath Road, Lymington. SO41 3SE

Royal Norfolk and Suffolk Yacht Club ....Royal Plain, Lowestoft. NR33 0AQ

Royal St George Yacht Club ....Dun Laoghaire, County Dublin, Eire.

Royal Victoria Yacht Club...............................91 Fishbourne Lane, Ryde, Isle of Wight. PO33 4EU

Royal Windermere Yacht Club ....Fallbarrow Road, Bowness-on-Windermere. LA33 3DJ

St Helier Yacht Club.......................................South Pier, St Helier, Jersey. JE2 3NB

West Mersea Yacht Club.................................116 Coast Road, West Mersea, Colchester. CO5 8PB

Royal Yachting Association ....RYA House, Ensign Way, Hamble-le-Rice, Southampton, Hampshire. SO31 4YA

DEFACED RAF ENSIGN

TThe RAF Sailing Association...........................HQ Air Command, RAF High Wycombe. HP14 4UE

ROYAL NAVAL RESERVE AND OTHER VESSELS AUTHORISED TO FLY THE BLUE ENSIGN IN MERCHANT VESSELS (FOREIGN OR HOME TRADE ARTICLES) AND FISHING VESSELS

1. A list of Royal Naval Reserve and other vessels authorised to fly the Blue Ensign will not be published in the Navy Directory.

2. Its inclusion in the Navy List was intended for the information of Captains of Her Majesty's Ships with reference to provisions of Article 9153 of the Queen's Regulations for the Royal Navy BRd 2 under which they are authorised to ascertain whether British Merchant Ships (including Fishing Vessels) flying the Blue Ensign of Her Majesty's Fleet are legally entitled to do so.

3. However, the usefulness of this list serves only a limited purpose as the list of vessels that could fly the Blue Ensign can change frequently. British merchant ships and fishing vessels are allowed to wear the plain Blue Ensign under the authority of a special Warrant, subject to certain conditions being fulfilled, and which are outlined below.

4. Vessels registered on the British Registry of Shipping or the Registry of a relevant British possession may wear a plain Blue Ensign providing the master or skipper is in possession of a warrant issued by the Commander Maritime Reserves under the authority of the Secretary of State for Defence, and the additional conditions outlined below are fulfilled. The Blue Ensign is to be struck if the officer to whom the warrant was issued relinquishes command, or if the ship or vessel passes into foreign ownership and ceases to be a British ship as defined in Part 1 of the Merchant Shipping Act 1995 (MSA 1995).

   a. Vessels on Parts I, II and IV of the Register. The master must be an officer of the rank of lieutenant RN/RNR or Captain RM/RMR or above in the Royal Fleet Reserve or the maritime forces of a United Kingdom Overseas Territory or Commonwealth country of which Her Majesty is Head of State, or an officer on the Active or Retired Lists of any branch of the maritime reserve forces of these countries or territories.

   b. Vessels on Part II of the Register. This part of the Register is reserved for fishing vessels. The skipper must comply with the same criteria as for sub-clause 4.a. above, however the crew must contain at least four members, each of whom fulfils at least one of the following criteria:

   Royal Naval or Royal Marine reservists or pensioner Reservists or pensioners from a Commonwealth monarchy or United Kingdom Overseas Territory, Ex-ratings or Royal Marines who have completed twenty years service in the Reserves, members of the Royal Fleet Reserve.

5. Action on sighting a merchant ship wearing a Blue Ensign: The Commanding Officer of one of HM ships on meeting a vessel wearing the Blue Ensign may, in exercise of powers conferred by sections 5, 7 and 257 MSA 1995, send on board a commissioned officer to confirm that the criteria outlined above are being met in full. If it is found that the ship is wearing a Blue Ensign, without authority of a proper warrant, the ensign is to be seized, taken away and forfeited to the Sovereign and the circumstances reported to the Commander Maritime Reserves, acting on behalf of the Chief of Naval Personnel and Training/Second Sea Lord, who maintains the list of persons authorised to hold such warrants.

   However, if it is found that, despite the warrant being sighted, the ship is failing to comply with the criteria in some other particular, the ensign is not to be seized but the circumstances are to be reported to the Commander Maritime Reserves.

HM SHIPS BFPO NUMBERS

ALBION (LPD)
BFPO 204

AMBUSH (Astute)
BFPO 205

ARCHER (Archer)
BFPO 208

ARGYLL (Type 23)
BFPO 210

ARTFUL (Astute)
BFPO 213

ASTUTE (Astute)
BFPO 214

AUDACIOUS (Astute)
BFPO 216

BANGOR (Sandown)
BFPO 222

BITER (Archer)
BFPO 229

BLAZER (Archer)
BFPO 231

BLYTH (Sandown)
BFPO 221

BROCKLESBY (Hunt)
BFPO 241

BULWARK (LPD)
BFPO 243

CATTISTOCK (Hunt)
BFPO 251

CHARGER (Archer)
BFPO 252

CHIDDINGFOLD (Hunt)
BFPO 254

CLYDE (River)
BFPO 255

DARING (Type 45)
BFPO 270

DASHER (Archer)
BFPO 271

DAUNTLESS (Type 45)
BFPO 272

DEFENDER (Type 45)
BFPO 267

DIAMOND (Type 45)
BFPO 273

DRAGON (Type 45)
BFPO 268

DUNCAN (Type 45)
BFPO 269

ECHO (Echo)
BFPO 275

ENTERPRISE (Echo)
BFPO 276

EXAMPLE (Archer)
BFPO 281

EXPLOIT (Archer)
BFPO 285

EXPLORER (Archer)
BFPO280

EXPRESS (Archer)
BFPO 282

FORTH
BFPO 286

GRIMSBY (Sandown)
BFPO 292

HURWORTH (Hunt)
BFPO 300

IRON DUKE (Type 23)
BFPO 309

KENT (Type 23)
BFPO 318

LANCASTER (Type 23)
BFPO 323

LEDBURY (Hunt)
BFPO 324

MAGPIE
BFPO 328

MEDWAY
BFPO 332

MERSEY (River)
BFPO 334

MIDDLETON (Hunt)
BFPO 335

MONMOUTH (Type 23)
BFPO 338

MONTROSE (Type 23)
BFPO 339

NORTHUMBERLAND (Type 23)
BFPO 345

PEMBROKE (Sandown)
BFPO 357

PENZANCE (Sandown)
BFPO 358

PORTLAND (Type 23)
BFPO 361

PROTECTOR (Ice Patrol Ship)
BFPO 367

PUNCHER (Archer)
BFPO 362

PURSUER (Archer)
BFPO 363

PRINCE OF WALES (Carrier)
BFPO 364

QUEEN ELIZABETH (Carrier)
BFPO 365

QUORN (Hunt)
BFPO 366

RAIDER (Archer)
BFPO 377

RAMSEY (Sandown)
BFPO 368

RANGER (Archer)
BFPO 369

RICHMOND (Type 23)
BFPO 375

SABRE (Scimitar)
BFPO 378

SCIMITAR (Scimitar)
BFPO 384

SCOTT (OSS)
BFPO 381

SEVERN (River)
BFPO 382

SHOREHAM (Sandown)
BFPO 386

SMITER (Archer)
BFPO 387

SOMERSET (Type 23)
BFPO 395

ST ALBANS (Type 23)
BFPO 399

SUTHERLAND (Type 23)
BFPO 398

TALENT (Trafalgar)
BFPO 401

TIRELESS (Trafalgar)
BFPO 402

TORBAY (Trafalgar)
BFPO 403

TRACKER (Archer)
BFPO 409

TRENCHANT (Trafalgar)
BFPO 405

TRIUMPH (Trafalgar)
BFPO 406

TRUMPETER (Archer)
BFPO 407

TURBULENT (Trafalgar)
BFPO 408

TYNE (River)
BFPO 412

VANGUARD (Vanguard)
BFPO 418

VENGEANCE (Vanguard)
BFPO 421

VICTORIOUS (Vanguard)
BFPO 419

VIGILANT (Vanguard)
BFPO 420

WESTMINSTER (Type 23)
BFPO 426

GLOSSARY OF ABBREVIATIONS
USED WITHIN THE NAVY DIRECTORY
ABBREVIATIONS OF RANKS USED BY JPA

Adm	Admiral
Adm of Fleet	Admiral of The Fleet
Brig	Brigadier
Cdre	Commodore
Chpln of The Fleet	Chaplain of The Fleet
Gen	General
Lt Gen	Lieutenant General
Maj Gen	Major General
R Adm	Rear Admiral
RN Prncpl Chpln	Principal Chaplain, Royal Navy
Surg Cdre	Surgeon Commodore
Surg V Adm	Surgeon Vice Admiral
V Adm	Vice Admiral

LIST OF BRANCH ABBREVIATIONS

Ch S	Chaplaincy Service
CS	Careers Service
DENTAL	Dental
ENG	Engineering
LOGS	Logistics
MED	Medical
QARNNS	Queen Alexandra's Royal Naval Nursing Service
RM	Royal Marines
RMR	Royal Marines Reserve
RNR	Royal Naval Reserve
WAR	Warfare

LIST OF MAIN TRADE ABBREVIATIONS

AAWO	Anti-Air Warfare Officer
AE	Air Engineer
AE O	Air Engineer Observer
AE P	Air Engineer Pilot
Anaes	Anaesthetics
ATC (RES)	Air Traffic Controller (Reserve)
ATC UT	Air Traffic Controller Under Training
AV	Aviation
AW (RES)	Above Water (Reserve)
AWO (U)	Advanced Warfare Officer (Underwater)
BPS	Burns & Plastic Surgeon
BS	Royal Marines Band Service

C .... Communications
C (SCC) ....Communications (Senior Corps Commission)
CS .... Careers Service
Dent (Cons) .... Dental Consultant
EM (C&S) ....Emergency Medicine (Command & Staff)
EM (Cons) ....Emergency Medicine (Consultant)
EN .... Emergency Nurse
FC .... Fighter Controller
GDMO .... General Duties Medical Officer
GDP .... General Dental Practitioner
GDP (VDP) .... General Dental Practitioner (Vocational Dental Practitioner)
GMP .... General Medical Practitioner
GS .... General Service (Royal Marines)
GS (Cons) .... General Surgeon (Consultant)
GSX .... General Service Warfare
H ....Hydrographic
HM .... Hydrographic Meteorological Oceanographic
HM (H CH) ....Hydrographic Meteorological (Hydrographic Charge)
HM (M CH) .... Hydrographic Meteorological (Meteorological Oceanographic Charge)
HM METOC (RES) ....Hydrographic Meteorological Oceanographic (Reserve)
HM(AM) ....Hydrographic Meteorological Oceanographic (Advanced Meteorologist)
HM(AS) .... Hydrographic Meteorological Oceanographic (Advanced Surveyor)
HW ....Heavy Weapons
HW (M) .... Heavy Weapons (Mortar)
Infection C .... Infection Control
INFO OPS (RES) ....Information Operations (Reserve)
INT ....Intelligence
IS .... Information Systems
IS(SM) .... Information System (Submarine)
ITU .... Intensive Therapy Unit
L .... Logistics
L BAR ....Logistics Barrister
L BAR SM .... Logistics Barrister Submarine
L CMA ....Logistics Cost Management Accountant
L CMA SM ....Logistics Cost Management Accountant Submarine
L FS ....Logistics Family Services
L SM ....Logistics Submarines
LC .... Landing Craft
MCD ....Minewarfare Clearance Diver
ME .... Marine Engineering
Med .... Medical
MEDIA OPS (RES) .... Media Operations (Reserve)
MESM ....Marine Engineering Submarine
METOC ....Meteorology & Oceanography
MH .... Mental Health
MLDR ....Mountain Leader
MS .... Medical Services

MS(CDO) ....Medical Services (Commando Trained)
MS(EHO)..Medical Services (Environmental Health Officer)
MS(SM)..Medical Services (Submarine)
MTO A (RES)..Maritime Trade Operations AWNIS (Reserve)
MTO A N (RES)........................Maritime Trade Operations AWNIS NCAGS (Reserve)
MTO N (RES) ....Maritime Trade Operations NCAGS (Reserve)
MW ....Mine Warfare
O ....Observer
O ASAC ....Observer Airborne Surveillance and Control
O LYNX...Observer Lynx
O MER ....Observer Merlin
O PWO(U)............................Observer Principal Warfare Officer (Underwater)
O SK6..Observer Sea King 6
O SKW...Observer Sea King AEW
O UT...Observer Under Training
Occ Med...Occupational Medicine
OMFS ....Oral & Maxillofacial Surgery
OP INT (RES)..Operational Intelligence (Reserve)
Ophthal ....Ophthalmology
ORL ....Otorhinolaryngologist
OT ....Operating Theatres
P...Pilot
P FW...Pilot Fixed Wing
P GAZ...Pilot Gazelle
P HELO PWO...............................Pilot Helicopter Principal Warfare Officer
P LYN7...Pilot Lynx 7
P LYNX ....Pilot Lynx
P MER...Pilot Merlin
P MER CDO ....Pilot Merlin Commando
P SK4..Pilot Sea King 4
P SK6..Pilot Sea King 6
P SKW...Pilot Sea King AEW
P UT...Pilot Under Training
Path - Haem...Pathology Haematology
Path – Micro ....Pathology Microbiology
PHC ....Primary Health Care
Psych ....Psychiatry
PWO...Principal Warfare Officer
PWO(A) ....Principal Warfare Officer (Above Water)
PWO(C) ....Principal Warfare Officer (Communications)
PWO(N) ....Principal Warfare Officer (Navigation)
PWO(SM)......................................Principal Warfare Officer (Submarine)
PWO(U) ....Principal Warfare Officer (Underwater)
REG ....Regulator
SCC ....Senior Corps Commission
SM(AWC) ....Submarine (Advanced Warfare Course)
SM(CQ)...Submarine (Command Qualified)

SM(N) .... Submarine (Navigator)
SM(X) .... Submarine (Warfare)
T&O ....Trauma & Orthopaedics
TM.. Training Manager
WE ....Weapons Engineering
WESM .... Weapons Engineer Submarine
WESM(SWS) .... Weapons Engineering Submarine (Strategic Weapons Systems)
WESM(TWS) .... Weapons Engineering Submarine (Tactical Weapons Systems)

ABBREVIATIONS OF ORGANISATIONS WHERE OFFICERS SERVE
WHEN NOT AT SEA

1 ACC ....1 Air Control Centre
1 ASSLT GP RM.. 1 Assault Group Royal Marines
1 IG ....1st Battalion Irish Guards
1 PWRR .... 1st Battalion Princess of Wales Royal Regiment
1 REGT AAC .... 1 Regiment Army Air Corps
1 RIFLES... 1st Battalion the Rifles
10 TRG SQN 1 ASSLT GP RM ....10 Training Squadron, 1 Assault Group Royal Marines
11 (ATT) SQN.................................. 11 (Amphibious Trials & Training) Squadron, Royal Marines
101 LOG BDE...101 Logistics Brigade
102 LOG BDE...102 Logistics Brigade
148 FO BTY RA.............. 148 (Meiktila) Commando Forward Observation Battery Royal Artillery
15 POG.. 15 Psychological Operations Group
1SL/CNS... First Sea Lord & Chief of Naval Staff
2SL CNPT....................Second Sea Lord and Chief of Naval Personnel & Training
202 SQN – E FLT .... E Flight, 202 Squadron Royal Air Force
26 REGT RA..26 Regiment, Royal Artillery
29 CDO REGT... 29 Commando Regiment
3 CDO BDE RM..3 Commando Brigade Royal Marines
3 FTS ....3 Flying Training School
3 REGT AAC .... 3 Regiment Army Air Corps
30 CDO IX GP RM.....................30 Commando Information Exploitation Group Royal Marines
4 REGT AAC .... 4 Regiment Army Air Corps
40 CDO RM..40 Commando Royal Marines
42 CDO RM..42 Commando Royal Marines
45 CDO RM..45 Commando Royal Marines
5 REGT AAC ....5 Regt Army Air Corps
5 SCOTS .... 5th Battalion the Royal Regiment of Scotland
539 ASSLT SQN RM .... 539 Assault Squadron Royal Marines
6 OPS SQN...6 Operations Squadron
6 SQN TYPHOON ....6 Squadron TYPHOON
7 AA BN REME........................ 7 Air Assault Battalion Royal Electrical & Mechanical Engineers
AACen.. Army Aviation Centre
ACHQ..Air Command Headquarters
ACDS(Nuc & Chem, Bio) ....Assistant Chief of Defence Staff (Nuclear & Chemical, Biological)

ACNS(A&C) .... Assistant Chief of Naval Staff (Aviation & Carriers)
ACNS(Cap) .... Assistant Chief of Naval Staff (Capability)
ACNS(Pers)/NAVSEC .... Assistant Chief of Naval Staff (Personnel) & Naval Secretary
ACNS(Pol) .... Assistant Chief of Naval Staff (Policy)
AFCC .... Armed Forces Chaplaincy Centre
AIB .... Admiralty Interview Board
ARF .... Aviation Reconnaissance Force
ARRC .... Allied Rapid Reaction Corps
ASG RM .... Armoured Support Group, Royal Marines
AWC .... Air Warfare Centre
BDS .... British Defence Section
BF BIOT .... British Forces British Indian Ocean Territory
BF C .... British Forces Cyprus
BF G .... British Forces Germany
BF GIBRALTAR .... British Forces Gibraltar
BFSAI .... British Forces South Atlantic Islands
BFPO .... British Forces Post Office
BMATT .... British Military Attache
BMM .... British Military Mission
BRNC .... Britannia Royal Naval College
CATCS .... Central Air Traffic Control School
CATD .... Combined Arms Tactics Division
CDI .... Chief of Defence Intelligence
CDO LOG REGT RM .... Commando Logistics Regiment Royal Marines
CFPS .... Commander, Fishery Protection Squad
CGRM .... Commandant General Royal Marines
CHF HQ .... Commando Helicopter Force, Headquarters
CJO .... Chief of Joint Operations
CoM(Fleet)/CFS .... Chief of Materiel (Fleet) and Chief of Fleet Support
COM(Ops) .... Commander, Operations
COMPORFLOT .... Commodore, Portsmouth Flotilla
COMUKAMPHIBFOR .... Commander UK Amphibious Forces
COMUKMARFOR .... Commander UK Maritime Forces
COMUKTG .... Commander United Kingdom Task Group
COS CC MAR FOR .... Chief of Staff to the Commander, Allied Naval Forces, Southern Europe
COS (Ops) PJHQ .... Chief of Staff (Operations) Permanent Joint Headquarters
COS SACT .... Chief of Staff to Supreme Allied Commander, Transformation
CSSE .... Chief Strategic Systems Executive
CTCRM .... Commando Training Centre Royal Marines
DCAE .... Defence College of Aeronautical Engineering
DCBRNC .... Defence Chemical, Biological, Radiological & Nuclear Centre
DCCIS .... Defence College of Communications & Information Systems
DCDS .... Deputy Chief of Defence Staff
DCEME ....Defence College of Electro-Mechanical Engineering
DCLPA .... Defence College of Logistics & Personnel Administration
DCMH ....Department of Community Mental Health
DCNS.. Deputy Chief of Naval Staff

DCOS Force Readiness .... Deputy Chief of Staff, Force Readiness
DCPG .... Defence College of Police & Guarding
DCSU...Defence Cultural Specialist Unit
DDG EUMS ....Deputy Director General, European Union Military Staff
DDS...Defence Dental Services
DE&S .... Defence Equipment & Support
DEFENCE ACADEMY....................................... Defence Academy of the United Kingdom
Def Reform (Mar) ITL.........................Defence Reform (Maritime) Implementation Team Leader
DEMSS....................................Defence Explosive Ordnance Disposal Munitions & Search School
DEPCOMSTRIKFORNATO ....Deputy Commander Strike Force NATO
DHFS .... Defence Helicopter Flying School
DIO.. Defence Infrastructure Organisation
D(MarCap & Transformation) /CofN .... Director (Maritime Capability & Transformation) and
Controller of the Navy
DMG ....Defence Medical Group
DMLS...Defence Maritime Logistics School
DMOC ....Defence Media Operations Centre
DMRC... Defence Medical Rehabilitation Centre
DMS ....Defence Medical Services
DMSTG... Defence Medical Services Training Group
DPMD..Defence Post-Graduate Medical Deanery
DSAS ....Defence Security & Assurance Services
DSEA ....Defence Safety and Environment Authority
DSL...Defence School of Languages
DST...Defence School of Transport
DST..Defence Science & Technology Laboratory
DTOEES .... Defence Technical Officer & Engineer Entry Scheme
ETPS .... Empire Test Pilots' School
EU OHQ...European Union Operational Headquarters
FCO .... Foreign & Commonwealth Office
FDS...Fleet Diving Squadron
FOSNI ....Flag Officer Scotland & Northern Ireland
FOST...Flag Officer Sea Training
FPGRM .... Fleet Protection Group Royal Marines
FWO .... Fleet Waterfront Organisation
HMNB.. Her Majesty's Naval Base
HQ 2 MED BDE...HQ 2 Medical Brigade
HQ EUFOR (SAR)...HQ European Force (Sarajevo)
HQ IADS ....HQ Integrated Area Defence System
HQ NI .... HQ Northern Ireland
HQLF .... HQ Land Forces
IBS .... Infantry Battle School
IMATT.. International Military Advisory & Training Team
INM .... Institute of Naval Medicine
JCTTAT ....Joint Counter Terrorism Training & Advisory Team
JEFTS ....Joint Elementary Flying Training School
JFC .... Joint Forces Command

JHC	Joint Helicopter Command
JSCSC	Joint Services Command & Staff College
JSMTC	Joint Services Mountain Training Centre
JSSU	Joint Services Signals Unit
JSU	Joint Support Unit
LATCC(MIL)	London Air Traffic Control Centre (Military)
LSP	Loan Service Position
LWC	Land Warfare Centre
MAA	Military Aviation Authority
MASF	Maritime Aviation Support Force
MCM1	Mine Countermeasures Squadron 1
MCM2	Mine Countermeasures Squadron 2
MCTC	Military Corrective Training Centre
MHRF(F)	Military High Readiness Force (France)
MOD	Ministry of Defence
MSSG	Military Stabilisation Support Group
MWC	Maritime Warfare Centre
MWS	Maritime Warfare School
NAIC	Naval Aeronautical Information Centre
NAS	Naval Air Squadron
NATO	North Atlantic Treaty Organisation
NATO JFC	NATO Joint Force Command
NATO JWC	NATO Joint Warfare Centre
NCHQ	Navy Command HQ
NCISS	NATO Communication & Information Systems School
NDG	Northern Diving Group
NETS	Naval Educational & Training Service
NOC	Naval Outdoor Centre
NRC EE & CRF	Naval Regional Commander Eastern England & Commander Regional Forces
NRC NE	Naval Regional Commander Northern England
NRC SNI	Naval Regional Commander Scotland & Northern Ireland
NRC WWE	Naval Regional Commander Wales & Western England
OCLC	Officer Career Liaison & Recruiting Officer
OPTAG	Operational Training & Advisory Group
PJHQ	Permanent Joint HQ
RBAF	Royal Brunei Armed Forces
RCDM	Royal Centre for Defence Medicine
RCDS	Royal College of Defence Studies
RM BICKLEIGH	Royal Marines, Bickleigh, Plymouth
RM CHIVENOR	Royal Marines, Chivenor, Barnstaple
RM CONDOR	Royal Marines Condor, Arbroath
RM NORTON MANOR	Royal Marines Norton Manor Camp, Taunton
RM POOLE	Royal Marines Hamworthy, Poole
RM STONEHOUSE	Royal Marines Stonehouse, Plymouth
RMSM	Royal Marines School of Music
RMAS	Royal Military Academy Sandhurst
RMBS	Royal Marine Band Service

RNAC .... Royal Naval Acquaint Centre
RNAESS .... Royal Naval Air Engineering & Survival School
RNAS .... Royal Naval Air Station
RNCR .... Royal Naval Centre of Recruiting
RNEAWC .... Royal Naval Element Air Warfare Centre
RNIO .... Royal Naval Infrastructure Organisation
RNLA .... Royal Naval Leadership Academy
RNLO .... Royal Navy Liaison Officer
RNLT .... Royal Navy Liaison Team
RNPT .... Royal Navy Presentation Team
RNSME .... Royal Naval School of Marine Engineering
RNSMS .... Royal Navy Submarine School
SACT .... Supreme Allied Commander, Transformation
SDG .... Southern Diving Unit Group
SETT .... Submarine Escape Training Tank
SGD .... Surgeon General's Department
SHAPE .... Supreme Headquarters Allied Powers Europe
SHTC .... Salmond House Training Centre
SMC .... Sea Mounting Centre
SP WPNS SCH .... Support Weapons School
SPVA .... Service Personnel & Veterans Agency
UKHO .... United Kingdom Hydrographic Office
UKJSU .... United Kingdom Joint Support Unit
UK MCC .... United Kingdom Maritime Component Commander
UKTI-DSO .... United Kingdom Trade & Investment Defence & Security Organisation
UN .... United Nations
US CENTCOM .... United States Central Command

Explanatory Notes
1. Any Officer who has the unit MCM1 or MCM2 will be assigned to one of the two Mine Countermeasure Squadrons and will be part of a rotating squad assigned to the Hunt & Sandown Class Mine Countermeasure vessels.
2. The location stated in the list of addresses may not necessarily be the Headquarters of that unit; it may simply be a location where an officer is serving.
3. Any Officer serving in a Defence Section, Exchange Post, Loan Service, Military Mission or Service Attache position, can be contacted by using the 'Yellow' book, as detailed on page 69

ADDRESSES OF ORGANISATIONS WHERE OFFICERS SERVE WHEN NOT AT SEA

NAVAL STAFF & NAVY COMMAND HEADQUARTER FUNCTIONS

First Sea Lord & Chief of Naval Staff
1SL/CNS
Ministry of Defence
Main Building
LONDON
SW1A 2HB

Fleet Commander
Mail Point 2.1
Leach Building
Whale Island
PORTSMOUTH
PO2 8BY

Second Sea Lord/Deputy Chief of Naval Staff
Mail Point 2.1
Leach Building
Whale Island
PORTSMOUTH
PO2 8BY

Admiralty Interview Board
AIB
HMS Sultan
GOSPORT
PO12 3BY

Commander Operations
COM(Ops)
Maritime Operations Centre
Oswald Building
Northwood HQ
Sandy Lane
NORTHWOOD
HA6 3AP

Commander UK Amphibious Forces
COMUKAMPHIBFOR
Whale Island
PORTSMOUTH
PO2 8ER

Commander UK Maritime Forces
COMUKMARFOR
Fieldhouse Building
Whale Island
PORTSMOUTH
PO2 8ER

Commander Amphibious Task Group
COMATG
No 6 House
RM Barracks
Stonehouse
PLYMOUTH
Devon
PL1 3QS

Commander UK Carrier Strike Group
COMUKCSG
The Parade
HMNB
PORTSMOUTH
PO1 3NB

Chaplain of the Fleet
Naval Chaplaincy Service
Navy Command HQ
Leach Building
Whale Island
PORTSMOUTH
PO2 8BY

Assistant Chief of Naval Staff Submarines & Flag Officer Scotland & Northern Ireland
ACNS SM & FOSNI
Command Building
HMNB Clyde
FASLANE
Argyll & Bute
G84 8HL

Commander Core Naval Training (COMCORE)
FOST
Raleigh Block
HMS Drake
HMNB Devonport
PLYMOUTH
PL2 2BG

Commander Operational Training (COMOT)
FOST
COMOT HQ
Vernon Building
HMS Collingwood
Newgate Lane
FAREHAM
PO14 1AS

Flag Officer Sea Training (North)
FOST (North)
Sea Training Building
HMNB Clyde
FASLANE
Helensburgh
G84 8HL

Flag Officer Sea Training (South)
FOST (South)
Grenville Block
HMS Drake
HMNB Devonport
PLYMOUTH
PL2 2BG

Fleet Diving Squadron
FDS
Horsea Island
West Bund Road
COSHAM
PO6 4TT

Headquarters Combined Cadet Force (Royal Navy)
CCF HQ (RN)
Room 3 Building 1/80
PP 73A
HMNB
PORTSMOUTH
PO1 3LU

Headquarters Sea Cadet Corps
SCC HQ
202 Lambeth Road
LONDON
SE1 7JW

Commander Regional Forces
CRF
Whale Island
PORTSMOUTH
Hampshire
PO2 8ER

Naval Regional Commander Eastern England
NRC EE
HMS President Medway Tender
Collingwood Block
Brompton Barracks
Khyber Road
CHATHAM
ME4 4TT

Naval Regional Commander Northern England and the Isle of Man
NRC NE
Naval Regional Headquarters Northern England and Isle of Man
HMS Eaglet
80 Sefton Street
East Brunswick Dock
LIVERPOOL
L3 4DZ

Naval Regional Commander for Scotland & Northern Ireland
NRC SNI
Naval Regional Headquarters Scotland and Northern Ireland
MOD CALEDONIA
Hilton Road
Rosyth
KY11 2XH

**Naval Regional Commander for Wales and
Western England**
NRC WWE
Naval Regional Headquarters Wales and Western
England
HMS FLYING FOX
Winterstoke Road
BRISTOL
BS3 2NS

SHORE BASES, ESTABLISHMENTS & OTHER NAVY ORGANISATIONS

Commander Fishery Protection Squadron
CFPS
HMNB
PORTSMOUTH
PO1 3LR

COMMANDER DEVONPORT FLOTILLA
COMDEVFLOT
HMNB DEVONPORT
PLYMOUTH
Devon
PL2 2BG

COMMANDER PORTSMOUTH FLOTILLA
COMPORFLOT
HMNB PORTSMOUTH
PORTSMOUTH
Hants
PO1 3LS

COMMANDER FASLANE FLOTILLA
COMFASFLOT
HMNB CLYDE
Faslane
HELENSBURGH
Argyll and Bute
G84 0EH

Her Majesty's Naval Base Clyde
HMNB CLYDE
Faslane
HELENSBURGH
Argyll and Bute
G84 0EH

Her Majesty's Naval Base Devonport
HMNB DEVONPORT
PLYMOUTH
Devon
PL2 2BG

Her Majesty's Naval Base Portsmouth
HMNB PORTSMOUTH
PORTSMOUTH
Hants
PO1 3LS

HMS Bristol
Whale Island
PORTSMOUTH
PO2 8ER

HMS Caledonia
Hilton Road
ROSYTH
Dunfermline
KY11 2EX

HMS Collingwood
Newgate Lane
FAREHAM
PO14 1AS

HMS Drake
HMNB DEVONPORT
PLYMOUTH
Devon
PL2 2BG

HMS Excellent
Whale Island
PORTSMOUTH
PO2 8ER

HMS Nelson
HMNB PORTSMOUTH
Queen Street
PORTSMOUTH
PO1 3HH

HMS Neptune
HMNB CLYDE
Faslane
HELENSBURGH
Argyll & Bute
G84 8HL

HMS President
72 St Katharine's Way
Tower Hamlets
LONDON
E1W 1UQ

HMS Sultan
Military Road
GOSPORT
PO12 3BY

HMS Temeraire
Burnaby Road
PORTSMOUTH
PO1 2HB

HMS Victory
HMNB PORTSMOUTH
PORTSMOUTH
PO1 3NH

Maritime Aviation Support Force
MASF
RNAS Culdrose
HELSTON
TR12 7RH

Maritime Warfare Centre
MWC
HMS Collingwood
Newgate Lane
FAREHAM
PO14 1AS

Naval Aeronautical Information Centre
NAIC
RAF Northolt
West End Road
RUISLIP
Middlesex
HA4 6NG

Officer Career Liaison & Recruiting Offices
OCLC
HMS Forward
42 Tilton Road
BIRMINGHAM
B9 4PD

Officer Career Liaison & Recruiting Offices
OCLC
21-23 Hereward Centre
PETERBOROUGH
PE1 2NJ

Officer Career Liaison & Recruiting Offices
OCLC
Pilgrim House
Derry's Cross
PLYMOUTH
PL1 2SW

Officer Career Liaison & Recruiting Offices
OCLC
Albion Wharf
19 Albion Street
MANCHESTER
M1 5LN

Royal Naval Air Station Culdrose
RNAS Culdrose
HMS Seahawk
HELSTON
TR12 7RH

Home to:
736, 750, 814, 820, 824, 829, 849 Naval Air Squadrons

Royal Naval Air Station Prestwick
RNAS Prestwick
HMS Gannet
PRESTWICK
KA9 2RR

Royal Naval Air Station Yeovilton
RNAS Yeovilton
HMS Heron
YEOVIL
BA22 8HT
Home to:
727, 815, 825, 845, 846, 847, 848 Naval Air
Squadrons & Commando Helicopter Force HQ.

Royal Navy Presentation Team
RNPT
First Floor Offices
Admiralty House North Wing
HM Naval Base
PORTSMOUTH
PO1 3LR

Royal Navy Royal Marines Welfare Eastern & Overseas Hub
RNRMW (East)
HMS Nelson
HMNB
PORTSMOUTH
PO1 3HH

Royal Navy Royal Marines Welfare Western Hub
RNRMW (West)
HMS Drake
HMNB Devonport
PLYMOUTH
PL2 2BG

Royal Navy Royal Marines Welfare Scotland Hub
RNRMW (Scotland)
1-5 Churchill Square
HELENSBURGH
G84 9HL

Royal Navy Royal Marines Welfare Central Hub
RNRMW (Central)
Somerset Court
Royal Naval Air Station
Yeovilton
ILCHESTER
Somerset
BA22 8HT

Royal Navy & Royal Marines Welfare Hub
RNRMW Hub
Queen St
HMS Nelson
HMNB PORTSMOUTH
PO1 3HH

Wildcat Maritime Force HQ
Building 223
RNAS Yeovilton
ILCHESTER
Somerset
BA22 8HT

Wildcat Maritime Force Support Cell
RNAS Yeovilton
ILCHESTER
Somerset
BA22 8HT

ROYAL MARINES ESTABLISHMENTS AND UNITS

HQ 3 Commando Brigade Royal Marines
HQ 3 Cdo Bde RM
RM Stonehouse
Durnford
PLYMOUTH
PL1 3QS

1 Assault Group Royal Marines
1 Asst Gp RM
RM Tamar
Triumph Building
HMNB Devonport
PLYMOUTH
PL2 2BG

10 Training Squadron 1 Assault Group Royal Marines
10 Trg Sqn 1 Asst Gp RM
RM Tamar
HMNB Devonport
PLYMOUTH
PL2 2BG

11 (Amphibious Trials & Training) Squadron
11 (ATT) SQN
1 ASSLT GP RM
Instow
BIDEFORD
EX39 4JH

131 Commando Squadron Royal Engineers
131 Cdo Sqn RE
Army Reserve Centre
Honeypot Lane
Kingsbury
LONDON
NW9 9QF

148 (Meiktila) Commando Forward Observation Battery Royal Artillery
148 FO BTY RA
RM Poole
Hamworthy
POOLE
Dorset
BH15 4NQ

1st Battalion the Rifles
1 RIFLES
Beachley Barracks
CHEPSTOW
Gloucestershire
NP16 7YG

24 Commando Regiment Royal Engineers
24 Cdo Regt RE
RMB Chivenor
BARNSTAPLE
EX31 4AZ

29 Commando Regiment Royal Artillery
29 Cdo Regt RA
Royal Citadel
PLYMOUTH
PL1 2PD

30 Commando Information Exploitation Group Royal Marines
30 Cdo IX Gp RM
RM Stonehouse
PLYMOUTH
Devon
PL1 3QS

40 Commando Royal Marines
40 Cdo RM
Norton Manor Camp
TAUNTON
Somerset
TA2 6PF

42 Commando Royal Marines
42 Cdo RM
Bickleigh Barracks
PLYMOUTH
Devon
PL6 7AJ

43 Commando Fleet Protection Group Royal Marines
43 Cdo FPGRM
HMNB Clyde
Faslane
HELENSBURGH
Argyll & Bute
G84 8HL

45 Commando Group Royal Marines
45 Cdo Gp RM
RM Condor
ARBROATH
Angus
DD11 3SJ

539 Assault Squadron Royal Marines
539 Asst Sqn RM
RM Tamar
HMNB Devonport
PLYMOUTH
PL2 2BG

Armoured Support Group Royal Marines
ASGp RM
Yeovil Block,
RNAS Yeovilton
YEOVIL
Somerset
BA22 8HT

Headquarters Commando Helicopter Force
CHF HQ
RNAS Yeovilton
YEOVIL
Somerset
BA22 8HT

Commando Logistic Regiment Royal Marines
Cdo Log Regt RM
RMB Chivenor
BARNSTAPLE
Devon
EX31 4AZ

Commando Training Centre Royal Marines
CTCRM
Lympstone
EXMOUTH
Devon
EX8 5AR

Defence School of Electronic and Mechanical Engineering
DSEME
8 Training Battalion REME DSEME
MOD Lyneham
CHIPPENHAM
SN15 4XX

HASLER COMPANY
HMS Drake
PLYMOUTH
PL2 2BG

Headquarters Royal Marine Band Service
HQ BS RM
Walcheren Building
HMS Excellent
Whale Island
PORTSMOUTH
PO2 8ER

Royal Marines Band Collingwood
RM Band Collingwood
HMS Collingwood
FAREHAM
Hampshire
PO14 1AS

Royal Marines Band Portsmouth
RM Band Portsmouth
Eastney Block
HMS NELSON
Queen Street
PORTSMOUTH
PO1 3HH

Royal Marines Band Commando Training Centre Royal Marines
RM Band CTCRM
CTCRM
Lympstone
EXMOUTH
Devon
EX8 5AR

Royal Marines Band Plymouth
RM Band Plymouth
HMS RALEIGH
TORPOINT
Cornwall
PL11 2PD

Royal Marines Band Scotland
RM Band Scotland
HMS Caledonia
ROSYTH
Fife
Scotland
KY11 2XH

Royal Marines Bickleigh
RM Bickleigh
Bickleigh Barracks
PLYMOUTH
PL6 7AJ

Royal Marines Chivenor
RM Chivenor
RMB Chivenor
Braunton
BARNSTAPLE
Devon
EX31 4AZ

Royal Marines Condor
RM Condor
Battenberg Road
ARBROATH
Angus
DD11 3SP

Royal Marines Norton Manor
RM Norton Manor
Norton Manor Camp
TAUNTON
Somerset
TA2 6PF

Royal Marines Poole
RM Poole
Hamworthy
POOLE
BH15 4NQ

Royal Marines Stonehouse
RM Stonehouse
Stonehouse Barracks
Durnford St
PLYMOUTH
PL1 3QS

Royal Marines School of Music
RMSM
HMS NELSON
Queen Street
PORTSMOUTH
PO1 3HH

MEDICAL UNITS

Defence Dental Service
DDS
DMS Whittington
Whittington Barracks
Whittington
LICHFIELD
WS14 9PY

Defence Medical Rehabilitation Centre
DMRC
Headley Court
Headley
EPSOM
KT18 6JW

Defence Medical Services
DMS
Whittington Barracks
Whittington
LICHFIELD
WS14 9PY

Defence College of Healthcare Education and Training
DCHET
DMS Whittington
Whittington Barracks
Whittington
LICHFIELD
WS14 9PY

Defence Healthcare Education & Training
DHET
DMS Whittington
Whittington Barracks
Whittington
LICHFIELD
WS14 9PY

Department of Community Mental Health
DCMH
PP6
Sunny Walk
HMNB
PORTSMOUTH
PO1 3LT

HQ 2 Medical Brigade
HQ 2 MED BDE
Queen Elizabeth Barracks
Strensall
YORK
YO32 5SW

Institute of Naval Medicine
INM
Alverstoke
GOSPORT
PO12 2DL

Joint Hospital Group South West
JHG(SW)
L3 Norwich Union Building
Brest Road
Derriford
PLYMOUTH
PL6 5YE

Joint Hospital Group South East
JHG(SE)
Frimley Park Hospital
Portsmouth Road
FRIMLEY
GU16 7UJ

Joint Hospital Group North
JHG(N)
Friarage Hospital
NORTHALLERTON
DL7 9NJ

Joint Hospital Group South
JHG(S)
Queen Alexandra Hospital
Albert House
Southwick Hill Road
Cosham
PORTSMOUTH
PO6 3LY

Royal Centre for Defence Medicine
RCDM
Queen Elizabeth Hospital
Queen Elizabeth Medical Centre
Edgbaston
BIRMINGHAM
B15 2WB

Surgeon General's Department
SGD
Coltman House
DMS Whittington
Lichfield Barracks
Whittington
LICHFIELD
WS14 9PY

ROYAL NAVAL RESERVE & ROYAL MARINES RESERVE UNITS

ROYAL MARINES RESERVE UNITS

RMR Bristol
Dorset House
Litfield Place
Clifton Down
BRISTOL
BS8 3NA

RMR London
351 Merton Road
LONDON
SW18 5JX

RMR Merseyside
RNHQ Merseyside
Sefton Street
East Brunswick Dock
LIVERPOOL
L3 4DZ

RMR Scotland
37-51 Birkmyre Road
Govan
GLASGOW
G51 3JH

RMR Tyne
Anzio House
Quayside
NEWCASTLE-UPON-TYNE
NE6 1BU

ROYAL NAVAL RESERVE UNITS

HMS Calliope
(Including Ceres Division)
South Shore Road
GATESHEAD
NE8 2BE

HMS Cambria
Hayes Point
Hayes Lane
Sully
PENARTH
CF64 5XU

HMS Dalriada
37-39 Birkmyre Rd
Govan
GLASGOW
G51 3JH

HMS Eaglet
Naval Regional Headquarters
80 Sefton Street
Docklands
LIVERPOOL
L3 4DZ

HMS Ferret
Building 600
Chicksands
SHEFFORD
Bedford
SG17 5PR

HMS Flying Fox
Winterstoke Road
BRISTOL
BS3 2NS

HMS Forward
42 Tilton Road
BIRMINGHAM
B9 4PP

HMS Hibernia
Thiepval Barracks
Magheralave Road
LISBURN
BT28 3NP

HMS King Alfred
Fraser Building
Whale Island
PORTSMOUTH
PO2 8ER

HMS President
72 St Katharine's Way
LONDON
E1W 1UQ

HMS Scotia
(Including Tay Division)
MOD Caledonia
Hilton Road
ROSYTH
KY11 2XH

HMS Sherwood
RNR Training Centre
Foresters House
Swiney Way
Beeston
NOTTINGHAM
NG9 6GX

HMS Vivid
Building SO40A
HM Naval Base Devonport
PLYMOUTH
PL2 2BG

HMS Wildfire
Northwood Headquarters
Sandy Lodge Way
NORTHWOOD
Middlesex
HA6 3HP

ROYAL NAVAL RESERVE AIR BRANCH

Royal Naval Reserve Air Branch
Cormorant House
Yeovilton
YEOVIL
Somerset
BA22 8HL

UNIVERSITY ROYAL NAVAL UNITS

Birmingham University
Royal Naval Unit (HMS Exploit)
HMS Forward
42 Tilton Road
Garrison Lane
BIRMINGHAM
B9 4PP

Bristol University
Royal Naval Unit (HMS Dasher)
HMS Flying Fox
Winterstoke Road
BRISTOL
BS3 2UP

Cambridge University
Royal Naval Unit (HMS Trumpeter)
2 Chaucer Road
CAMBRIDGE
CB2 7EB

Edinburgh University
Royal Naval Unit (HMS Archer)
Hepburn House
89 East Claremount Street
EDINBURGH
EH7 4HU

Glasgow & Strathclyde University
Royal Naval Unit (HMS Pursuer)
95 University Place
GLASGOW
G12 8SU

Liverpool University
Royal Naval Unit (HMS Charger)
RN Headquarters
80 Sefton Street
East Brunswick Dock
LIVERPOOL
L3 4DZ

London University
Royal Naval Unit (HMS Puncher)
HMS President
72 St Katherine's Way
LONDON
EW1 1UQ

Manchester & Salford University
Royal Naval Unit (HMS Biter)
University Barracks
Boundary Lane
MANCHESTER
M15 6DH

Northumbrian University
Royal Naval Unit (HMS Example)
HMS Calliope
South Shore Road
GATESHEAD
NE8 2BE

Oxford University
Royal Naval Unit (HMS Smiter)
Falklands House
Oxpens Road
OXFORD
OX1 1RX

Southampton University
Royal Naval Unit (HMS Blazer)
Room 451/06
National Oceanographic Centre
Waterfront Campus
European Way
SOUTHAMPTON
SO14 3ZH

Sussex University
Royal Naval Unit (HMS Ranger)
Army Reserve Barracks
198 Dyke Road
BRIGHTON
East Sussex
BN1 5AS

Wales Universities
Royal Naval Unit (HMS Express)
HMS CAMBRIA
Hayes Point
Hayes Lane
Sully
PENARTH
South Glamorgan
CF64 5XU

Yorkshire & Humberside Universities
Royal Naval Unit (HMS Explorer)
HMS Ceres
Carlton Barracks
Carlton Gate
LEEDS
LS7 1HE

TRAINING ESTABLISHMENTS

Air Warfare Centre
AWC
RAF Waddington
LINCOLN
LN5 9NB

Armed Forces Chaplaincy Centre
AFCC
Amport House
Amport
ANDOVER
SP11 8BG

Army Aviation Centre
AACen
Middle Wallop
STOCKBRIDGE
SO20 8DY

Britannia Royal Naval College
BRNC
DARTMOUTH
TQ6 0HJ

Central Air Traffic Control School
CATCS
RAF Shawbury
SHREWSBURY
SY4 4DZ

Commando Training Centre Royal Marines
CTCRM
Lympstone
EXMOUTH
EX8 5AR

Defence Academy of the United Kingdom
Vincent Centre
Faringdon Road
SHRIVENHAM
SN6 8LA

Defence Chemical, Biological, Radiological & Nuclear Centre
Defence CBRN Centre
Winterbourne Gunner
SALISBURY
Wiltshire
SP4 0ES

Defence School of Aeronautical Engineering
DSAE
RAF Cosford
WOLVERHAMPTON
WV7 3EX

Defence School of Communications & Information Systems
DSCIS
HMS Collingwood
Newgate Lane
FAREHAM
PO14 1AS

Defence College of Communications & Information Systems
DCCIS
Blandford Camp
BLANDFORD FORUM
DT11 8RH

Defence School of Electro-Mechanical Engineering
DSEME
HMS Sultan
Military Road
GOSPORT
PO12 3BY

Defence College of Logistics, Policing and Administration HQ
DCLPA
Princess Royal Barracks
Deepcut
CAMBERLEY
Surrey
GU16 6RW

Defence School of Personnel Administration
DSPA
Worthy Down
WINCHESTER
SO21 2RG

Defence College of Police & Guarding
DCPG
Southwick Park
FAREHAM
PO17 6EJ

Defence Cultural Specialist Unit
DCSU
RAF Henlow
HITCHIN
Bedfordshire
SG16 6DN

Defence Diving School
DDS
Horsea Island
West Bund Road
COSHAM
PO6 4TT

Defence Explosive Ordnance Disposal Munitions & Search Training Regiment
DEMS Trg Regt
St George's Barracks
Arncott Wood Road
BICESTER
OX25 1PP

Defence Helicopter Flying School
DHFS
RAF Shawbury
SHREWSBURY
Shropshire
SY4 4DZ

Defence Maritime Logistics School
DMLS
HMS Raleigh
TORPOINT
PL11 2PD

Defence College of Healthcare Education & Training
DCHET
DMS Whittington
Whittington Barracks
Whittington
LICHFIELD
WS14 9PY

Defence Centre for Languages & Culture
DCLC
Defence Academy
SHRIVENHAM
SN6 8LA

Defence School of Marine Engineering
DSMarE
HMS Sultan
Military Road
GOSPORT
PO12 3BY

Defence School of Transport

DST
Normandy Barracks
Leconfield
BEVERLEY
East Yorkshire
HU17 7LX

Defence Technical Officer & Engineer Entry Scheme

DTOEES
Defence Academy of the United Kingdom
Vincent Centre
Faringdon Road
SHRIVENHAM
SN6 8LA

Defence Technical Officer & Engineer Entry Scheme

DTOEES
Aston & Brimingham Universities
HMS Forward
42 Tilton Road
BIRMINGHAM
B9 4PP

Defence Technical Officer & Engineer Entry Scheme

DTOEES
Loughborough University
Keith Green Building
LOUGHBOROUGH
LE11 3TU

Defence Technical Officer & Engineer Entry Scheme

DTOEES
Southampton University
Capella House
Cook Street
SOUTHAMPTON
SO14 1NJ

Defence Technical Officer & Engineer Entry Scheme

DTOEES
Newcastle and Northumbria Universities
HMS Calliope
South Shore Road
GATESHEAD
Tyne and Wear
NE8 2BE

Empire Test Pilots' School

ETPS
MOD Boscombe Down
SALISBURY
Wiltshire
SP4 0JF

HMS Raleigh

TORPOINT
PL11 2PD

Infantry Battle School

IBS
Dering Lines
BRECON
Powys
LD3 7RA

Institute of Naval Medicine

INM
Crescent Road
Alverstoke
GOSPORT
PO12 2DL

Joint Elementary Flying Training School

JEFTS
RAF Cranwell
SLEAFORD
Lincolnshire
NG34 8HB

Joint Forces Command Chicksands

JFC Chicksands
SHEFFORD
SG17 5PR

Joint Services Command & Staff College

JSCSC
Faringdon Road
Shrivenham
SWINDON
SN6 8TS

Joint Services Mountain Training Centre

JSMTC
Indefatigable
Plas Llanfair
Llanfair PG
ANGLESEY
LL61 6NT

Land Warfare Centre
LWC
Waterloo Lines
Imber Road
WARMINSTER
Wiltshire
BA12 0DJ

Maritime Warfare Centre
MWC
HMS Collingwood
Newgate Lane
FAREHAM
PO14 1AS

Maritime Warfare School
MWS
HMS Collingwood
Newgate Lane
FAREHAM
PO14 1AS

Naval Outdoor Centre Germany
NOC
Box 2021
SONTHOFEN
BFPO 105

Operational Training & Advisory Group
OPTAG
Risborough Barracks
Shorncliffe Camp
FOLKSTONE
CT20 3HW

Royal College of Defence Studies
RCDS
Belgrave Square
37 Upper Belgrave St
LONDON
SW1X 8NS

Royal Marines School of Music
RMSM
HMS Nelson
HMNB
PORTSMOUTH
PO1 3HH

Royal Military Academy Sandhurst
RMAS
Haig Road
CAMBERLEY
Surrey
GU15 4PQ

Royal Naval Air Engineering & Survival School
RNAESS
HMS Sultan
Military Road
GOSPORT
PO12 3BY

Royal Naval Element Air Warfare Centre
RNEAWC
RAF Waddington
LINCOLN
LN5 9NB

Royal Naval Leadership Academy
RNLA
HMS Collingwood
Newgate Lane
FAREHAM
PO14 1AS

Royal Naval Leadership Academy
RNLA
Ashford House
Britannia Royal Naval College
DARTMOUTH
TQ6 0HJ

Royal Naval School of Physical Training
RNSPT
HMS Temeraire
Burnaby Road
PORTSMOUTH
PO1 2HB

Royal Navy Pre-Deployment Training & Mounting Centre
RN PDTMC
HMS Nelson
HMNB
PORTSMOUTH
PO1 3HH

Royal Naval Centre of Recruiting
RNCR
Stanley Barracks
Bovington Camp
WAREHAM
BH20 6JA

Royal Navy Submarine School
RNSMS
HMS Raleigh
TORPOINT
PL11 2PD

Salmond House Training Centre
SHTC
Monchengladbach
Germany
BFPO 19

Specialist Weapons School
SP WPNS SCH
Waterloo Lines
Imber Road
WARMINSTER
Wiltshire
BA12 0DJ

MINISTRY OF DEFENCE DEPARTMENTS & ORGANISATIONS

Ministry of Defence
MOD
Main Building
Horse Guards Avenue
Whitehall
LONDON
SW1A 2HB

Chief of Joint Operations
Building 410
C G 209
JHQ NORTHWOOD
HA6 3HP

Defence Infrastructure Organisation Headquarters
DIO HQ
Kingston Road
SUTTON COLDFIELD
B75 7RL

Defence Infrastructure Organisation
DIO
RAF Wyton
Brampton and Wyton
HUNTINGDON
PE28 2EA

Defence Media Operations Centre
DMOC
RAF Halton
AYLESBURY
HP22 5PG

Defence Science & Technology Laboratory
DSTL
Headquarters
Porton Down
SALISBURY
SP4 0JQ

Defence Assurance & Information Security
DAIS
Bazalgette Pavilion
RAF Wyton
HUNTINGDON
Cambridgeshire
PE28 2EA

Defence Assurance & Information Security
DAIS
MOD Corsham
Westwells Road
CORSHAM
Wiltshire
SN13 9NR

UK Hydrographic Office
UKHO
Admiralty Way
TAUNTON
TA1 2DN

DEFENCE EQUIPMENT & SUPPORT ORGANISATIONS AND LOCATIONS

Defence Equipment & Support
DE&S
MOD Abbey Wood
BRISTOL
BS34 8JH

Defence Equipment & Support
DE&S
Gazelle House
RNAS YEOVILTON
ILCHESTER
Somerset
BA22 8HJ

Defence Equipment & Support
DE&S
Cormorant House
RNAS YEOVILTON
ILCHESTER
Somerset
BA22 8HL

Defence Equipment & Support
DE&S
Unicorn House
RNAS Yeovilton
ILCHESTER
Somerset
BA22 8HW

Defence Equipment & Support
DE&S
Basil Hill Site
MOD Corsham
Westwells Road
Box
CORSHAM
Wiltshire
SN13 9RA

Defence Equipment & Support
DE&S
3100 Massachusetts Avenue NW
WASHINGTON DC 20008
USA

Leonardo Helicopters
Lysander Road
YEOVIL
Somerset
BA20 2YB

BAE Sytems Maritime Submarines
BAE Systems Marine Ltd
Bridge Road
BARROW-IN-FURNESS
Cumbria
LA14 1AF

British Forces Post Office
BFPO
HQ BFPO
West End Road
RUISLIP
HA4 6DQ

UK Trade & Investment Defence & Security Organisation
UKTI-DSO
1 Victoria Street
LONDON
SW1H 0ET

Vector Aerospace
110 Fareham Road
GOSPORT
Hampshire
PO13 0AA

TRI-SERVICE UNITS

Allied Rapid Reaction Corps
ARRC
Imjin Barracks
INNSWORTH
Gloucester
GL3 1HW

British Forces British Indian Ocean Territory
BF BIOT
Diego Garcia
NP 1002
BFPO 485

British Forces Cyprus
BF C
BFPO 53

British Forces Gibraltar
BF GIBRALTAR
BFPO 52

British Forces Post Office
BFPO
HQ BFPO
West End Road
RUISLIP
HA4 6DQ

British Forces South Atlantic Islands
BFSAI
Falklands
BFPO 655

European Joint Support Unit (EJSU)
LISBON
Portugal
BFPO 6

HQ EUFOR
Camp Butmir
SARAJEVO
Boznia Herzegovina

HQ Integrated Area Defence System
HQ IADS
185 Jalan Ampang
50450 Kuala Lumpar
Malaysia

HQ Joint Forces Command Brunssum
Rimburgerweg 30
6445 PA Brunssum
Netherlands

Joint Counter Terrorism Training & Advisory Team
JCTTAT
Risborough Barracks
FOLKSTONE
Kent
CT20 3EZ

Joint Forces Command
JFC
Sandy Lane
NORTHWOOD
HA6 3HP

Joint Forces Command Chicksands
JFC Chicksands
SHEFFORD
SG17 5PR

Joint Helicopter Command
JHC
HQ Land Forces
Marlborough Lines
Monxton Road
ANDOVER
SP11 8HJ

Joint Service Signal Unit
JSSU
Ayios Nikolaos
CYPRUS
BFPO 59

Joint Service Signal Unit
JSSU
Hubble Road
CHELTENHAM
GL51 0EX

UK Joint Support Unit
UKJSU
LISBON
Portugal
BFPO 6

London Air Traffic Control Centre (Military)
LATCC(MIL)
Swanwick Centre
Sopwith Way
SWANWICK
Hampshire
SO31 7AY

Military Aviation Authority
MAA
MOD Abbey Wood
BRISTOL
BS34 8QW

Military Corrective Training Centre
MCTC
Berechurch Hall Camp
Berechurch Hall Road
COLCHESTER
Essex
CO2 9NU

Military High Readiness Force (France)
MHRF(F)
238 Avenue Auguste Batta
TOULON
France

NATO Supreme Allied Commander Transformation
NATO SACT
US Naval Base
NORFOLK
Virginia
NP 1964 via BFPO 63

NATO
Casteau
MONS
Belgium
BFPO 26

NATO HQ
BRUSSELS
Belgium
BFPO 49

NATO Allied Joint Forces Command Naples
NATO JFC
NAPLES
Italy
BFPO 8

NATO Joint Force Command Brunssum
NATO JFC
Holland
BFPO 28

NATO Joint Warfare Centre
NATO JWC
4068 STAVANGER
Norway
BFPO 50

NATO School
OBERAMMERGAU
Am Rainenbichl 54
82487 Oberammergau
Germany

Naval Striking and Support Forces NATO
STRIKFORNATO
Reduto Gomes Freire
Estrada da Medrosa
2780-070
Oeiras
Portugal

Permanent Joint Headquarters
PJHQ
Sandy Lane
NORTHWOOD
HA6 3AP

Royal Brunei Armed Forces
RBAF
Bolkiah Camp
BRUNEI
BFPO 11

Sea Mounting Centre
SMC
Marchwood
SOUTHAMPTON
SO40 4ZG

Veterans UK
Ministry of Defence
Norcross
Thornton
CLEVELEYS
FY5 3WP

Supreme HQ Allied Powers Europe
SHAPE
MONS
Belgium
BFPO 26

UK Mission to the United Nations
UN
P.O. Box 5238
NEW YORK
NY 10150-5238 USA

ARMY UNITS

HQ Land Forces
HQLF
Marlborough Lines
Monxton Road
ANDOVER
SP11 8HJ

1st Battalion Irish Guards
1IG
Cavalry Barracks
HOUNSLOW
London
TW4 6HD

1 Regt Army Air Corps
1 REGT AAC
RNAS Yeovilton
YEOVIL
Somerset
BA22 8HT

131 Independent Commando Squadron Royal Engineers (Volunteers)
131 INDEP CDO SQN RE (V)
Training Centre
Army Reserve Centre
Honeypot Lane
Kingsbury
LONDON
NW9 9QY

148 (Meiktila) Commando Forward Observation Battery Royal Artillery
148 FO BTY RA
RM Poole
Hamworthy
POOLE
BH15 4NQ

1st Battalion the Rifles
1 RIFLES
Beachley Road
Beachley Barracks
CHEPSTOW
NP16 7YG

101 Logistics Brigade & Signal Troop
101 Log Bde & Sig Tp
Buller Barracks
ALDERSHOT
GU11 2DE

102 Logistics Brigade
102 Log Bde
Prince Wm of Glos Barracks
1 Belvoir Ave
GRANTHAM
NG31 7TA

24 Commando Regiment Royal Engineers
24 Cdo Regt RE
RMB Chivenor
BARNSTAPLE
Devon
EX31 4AZ

26 Regiment Royal Artillery
26 Regt RA
Mansergh Barracks
GUTERSLOH
Germany
BFPO 47

29 Commando Regiment Royal Artillery
29 Cdo Regt RA
Royal Citadel
PLYMOUTH
Devon
PL1 2PD

3 Regiment Army Air Corps
3 Regt AAC
Wattisham Airfield
IPSWICH
Suffolk
IP7 7RA

4 Regiment Army Air Corps
4 Regt AAC
Wattisham Airfield
IPSWICH
Suffolk
IP7 7RA

5 Regiment Army Air Corps
5 REGT AAC
JHCFS ALDERGROVE
BFPO 808

5th Battalion Royal Regiment of Scotland
5 SCOTS
Redford Cavalry Barracks
265 Colinton Road
EDINBURGH
EH13 0PP

7 Air Assault Battalion, REME
7 AA BN REME
Wattisham Airfield
IPSWICH
Suffolk
IP7 7RA

Army Aviation Centre
AACen
Middle Wallop
STOCKBRIDGE
Hampshire
SO20 8DY

Army Recruiting & Training Division
ARTD
Trenchard Lines
Upavon
PEWSEY
Wiltshire
SN9 6BE

Royal Military Academy Sandhurst
RMAS
Haig Road
CAMBERLEY
Surrey
GU15 4PQ

ROYAL AIR FORCE UNITS

HQ Air Command
ACHQ
RAF High Wycombe
Walters Ash
HIGH WYCOMBE
Buckinghamshire
HP14 4UE

Control & Reporting Centre
CRC
RAF Boulmer
ALNWICK
Northumberland
NE66 3JF

202 Squadron, E Flight
202 SQN E Flight
Leconfield
BEVERLEY
East Yorkshire
HU17 7LX

Joint Helicopter Command Flying Station
JHFS
Aldergrove
BFPO 808

MOD Boscombe Down
SALISBURY
Wiltshire
SP4 0JF

MOD St Athan
BARRY
Vale of Glamorgan
CF62 4WA

RAF Barkston Heath
GRANTHAM
Lincolnshire
NG32 2DQ

RAF Benson
WALLINGFORD
Oxfordshire
OX10 6AA

RAF Boulmer
ALNWICK
Northumberland
NE66 3JF

RAF Brize Norton
CARTERTON
Oxfordshire
OX18 3LX

RAF College Cranwell
SLEAFORD
Lincolnshire
NG34 8HB

RAF Coningsby
Baxter Cl
Coningsby
LINCOLN
LN4 4TG

RAF Digby
LINCOLN
Lincolnshire
LN4 3LH

RAF Halton
AYLESBURY
Buckinghamshire
HP22 5PG

RAF Henlow
HENLOW
Bedfordshire
SG16 6DN

RAF High Wycombe
Walters Ash
HIGH WYCOMBE
Buckinghamshire
HP14 4UE

RAF Leeming
Gatenby
NORTHALLERTON
North Yorkshire
DL7 9NJ

RAF Linton-on-Ouse
YORK
North Yorkshire
YO30 2AJ

RAF Lossiemouth
LOSSIEMOUTH
Moray
IV31 6SD

RAF Northolt
West End Road
RUISLIP
London
HA4 6NG

RAF Odiham
HOOK
Hampshire
RG29 1QT

RAF Scampton
Scampton
LINCOLN
LN1 2ST

RAF Shawbury
SHREWSBURY
Shropshire
SY4 4DZ

RAF St Mawgan
NEWQUAY
Cornwall
TR8 4HP

RAF Valley
HOLYHEAD
Isle of Anglesey
LL65 3NY

RAF Waddington
LINCOLN
Lincolnshire
LN5 9NB

RAF Wattisham
IPSWICH
Suffolk
IP7 7RA

RAF Wittering
PETERBOROUGH
Cambridgeshire
PE8 6HB

RAF Wyton
Brampton and Wyton
HUNTINGDON
Cambridgeshire
PE28 2EA

RAF Wyton
Henlow
Bedfordshire
SG16 6DN

OTHER ADDRESSES

Ministry of Defence Guard Service
MGS
Wethersfield
BRAINTREE
Essex
CM7 4AZ

Ministry of Defence Police HQ
MDP HQ
Weathersfield
BRAINTREE
Essex
CM7 4AZ

Royal Navy & Royal Marines Charity
(Regn No. 1117794)
Registered Office:
Building 29
HMS Excellent
Whale Island
PORTSMOUTH
PO2 8ER

Marine Society & Sea Cadets HQ
MSSC
202 Lambeth Road
LONDON
SE1 7JW

The Cabinet Office
70 Whitehall
LONDON
SW1A 2AS

The Foreign & Commonwealth Office
King Charles Street
LONDON
SW1A 2AH

ATTACHES AND ADVISERS

The Defence Engagement Strategy Overseas Directory, commonly known as The Yellow Book, lists the UK MOD Attaché corps based at Defence Sections in British Embassies and High Commissions, together with Loan Service Personnel and Special Advisors Overseas. The Directory is maintained by the Defence Engagement Strategy Overseas Support Division. It is an extensive and comprehensive publication that is updated throughout the year on the Web and bi-annually in a limited run of hard copy (DESTRAT Overseas Directory (The DESTRAT Yellow Book)).

For access to Attaches and Advisers you should refer to these sources for accuracy.   A full and comprehensive listing of Attaches and Advisers can be accessed through the MoD intranet, the URL is:

https://modgovuk.sharepoint.com/sites/defnet/HOCS/Pages/DE-STRAT-Overseas-Directory---The-Yellow-Book.aspx

Hardcopy: Authorised users without ready access to the DefenceNet can obtain copies of the concise Directory on application to the Editor:

          Peter McCarney
          Defence Engagement-DALSC-Admin
          Main Building
          Level 4, Zone G, Desk 15
          Whitehall
          LONDON, SW1A 2HB.

MODNET: peter.mccarney781@mod.gov.uk (Official/Official-Sensitive)

Phone: 020 7218 9176

AMENDMENTS TO NAVY DIRECTORY ENTRY

This edition of the Navy Directory has been produced largely from the information held within the Ministry of Defence's "Joint Personnel and Administration" system". The efficiencies and data handling of JPA affect the way in which individual entries are extracted and recorded in the Navy Directory.

Serving Officers who note errors or omissions in the Navy Directory should ensure that their data held within JPA is accurate and up to date. If you are unable to make these corrections within your JPA account, you should seek assistance from either your JPA administrator or Career Manager.

Please note that all personnel data for the Navy Directory is derived through Career Managers/ Data Owners and/or extracted direct from JPA; it is neither compiled nor maintained by the Editor. If you notice errors or omissions, you should contact your Human Resources Manager.

All other errors or omissions should be brought to the attention of the Editor of the Navy Directory.

Readers who wish to comment on this edition of the Navy Directory are invited to write to:

> The Editor of the Navy Directory
> MP 2.2
> West Battery
> Whale Island
> PORTSMOUTH
> PO2 8DX

Service Number (mandatory) ....

Surname ....

Forenames ....

Rank ....

Comments:

Signed .... Date ....